T
ZODIAC CODE

God's Hidden Message in the Stars

F. Chris Patrick

The Zodiac Code
by F. Chris Patrick

ISBN 1-58169-133-5
For Worldwide Distribution
Printed in the U.S.A.

Gazelle Press
P.O. Box 191540
Mobile AL 36619
800-367-8203

TABLE OF CONTENTS

ACKNOWLEDGMENTS

My deepest gratitude to my dedicated wife, Leah, and my children who enabled me to spend many hours studying astronomy and this subject material.

My very special thanks to Wally and Sherry Marks who spent many long hours helping me to finish this book. Thanks to Barbara Funderburk for helping me proofread this material.

Special thanks to my Dad and Mom, along with the members of Life Church, whose prayers and support have made this book a reality.

The most special thanks to my Lord, Jesus Christ for saving me and revealing such wondrous things to the world.

Chapter One

Awakened to a Mystery

One dark, chilly night in January 1986, Halley's Comet started me on a journey searching for truth among the stars. Over 300 of us were gathered on a small island in the Gulf of Mexico to observe the comet through telescopes. My 81 year-old grandmother and her twin sister accompanied me that night. They had seen the comet years ago and were anxious to see it once again.

When our turn came at the telescopes, we weren't sure if we would see anything because of the overcast sky. Suddenly, the clouds parted and there it was... Halley's comet...but much more—the magnificent Milky Way! Everywhere I turned the telescope, I saw beautiful groups of stars. A sense of awe enveloped me and a strong desire was birthed in me to study the stars and find meaning in all that beauty.

After that night, I began reading everything about the stars I could find available. I joined an astronomy club and even bought myself a telescope. What I learned began to excite me. The signs of the Zodiac were not just interesting tales about mythical figures. I sensed a cosmic story was being told, written in the universal language of pictures for everyone to see in the sky. Since these stars were named so many thousands of years ago, I began to study all the ancient Scriptures found in the Bible pertaining to stars and constellations.

I found that the word "Zodiac" comes from the Hebrew word *zodi*, meaning "the way or path." I wanted to learn the path of these heavenly signs. Little did I know that I could come to understand the same mystery of the Zodiac that the Wise Men in the time of Christ had understood! I found the first mention of the stars in the book of Genesis.

> *And God said, Let there be lights in the firmament of the heaven to divide the day from the night; and let them be for signs, and for seasons, and for days, and years* (Genesis 1:14).

In doing any study in the Bible, looking up words in the original language enables us to get a better understanding of the meaning and usage of the word. So let's look at two words in the above scripture—signs "*oth*" and seasons "*moed*"—in the Hebrew and how they are used in the Bible. The word "*oth*" means "a signal of something to come." It also means "an ensign, standard or banner." In reading this book, you will see that part of the Zodiac Code involves the fact that God has hung banners in the heavens. One definition for *code* is "a system of symbols." The Zodiac has a three-part system (code) that, when understood, tells an amazing story.

The word for "season" is *moed,* which means something appointed or a fixed time and can also mean a signal as appointed beforehand (as for example a prophetic sign). It is never used for a season of the year (like winter), but is used when referring to a fixed time for a miraculous event. In Genesis 17:21, the word "*moed*" is used in a prophetic and miraculous way.

> *But my covenant I will establish with Isaac, whom Sarah will bear to you by this time* [moed] *next year* (Genesis 17:21).

Abraham was 100 years old and Sarah, his wife, was 90, so the birth of a son to this couple was indeed a miracle. It was also prophetic, because it was a predictive prophecy of what would happen a year in the future. *Moed* is used the same way in Genesis 18:14 and 21:2. Each refers to the supernatural fulfillment of the prophecy given about the birth of Isaac.

The stars are given to mankind to be for "signs and seasons" or "for signals of things to come (*oth*)" and "something appointed beforehand to happen at a fixed time (*moed*)." It is clear that God designed the stars with the purpose of using them prophetically to signify specific events in history that would come to pass at appointed times. For example, there is *Virgo*, the virgin woman. This constellation foretells that at a specific time in history a child would be born of a virgin.

This book will prove that astrology is nothing more than the perversion of the original use of the stars and constellations. I have become convinced that there has been a conspiracy to alter the true message of the stars by a being who is known by the names of Lucifer and Satan. He has used men throughout history to change, hide, misuse, and pervert this special prophetic knowledge given to us by God so we would not understand its message. It is also clear in the Bible that God condemns astrology. God is emphatic in his declaration that man is to abstain from this practice in Leviticus 18 and 19, Deuteronomy 18, and Isaiah 47:11-15. In fact, look at what God says in Amos 5:8:

> *Seek Him that maketh the seven stars and Orion...* (KJV).

We are to seek Him that made the stars and not seek the stars themselves for guidance. Astrology books appeal to the human psyche with promises for directions about such things as: knowing your own children, understanding your mate better, having more control over your own destiny, discovering lucky lotto numbers, and knowing your future. They also answer questions you may have, such as: What is ahead for your love life? When are you most likely to fall in and out of love? Which month is best to make money? Will your good health continue, or should you guard against illness or injury?

Astrology can be regarded as nothing less than occultic. It is an attempt to help gain knowledge of the future and an attempt to help better one's self apart from the God of the Bible. Only God knows the future, and He says it can be a good future. A lot depends on our choices. God sets before us life and death, the blessing or the curse.

> *"For I know the plans I have for you," declares the LORD, "plans to prosper you and not to harm you, plans to give you hope and a future"* (Jeremiah 29:11).

> *I call heaven and earth to record this day against you, that I have set before you life and death, blessing and cursing; therefore choose life, that both thou and thy seed may live* (Deuteronomy 30:19).

The astrologer tries to tell the future by the stars and planets when only God is the true source of the future, the past, and the present. Many who practice astrology move on to other new age occultic "guidance" methods, such as channeling and seances. While some astrologers claim that their talents and abilities are a gift from God, He would never give as a "gift" what He calls an abomination. So the first Bible clue tells us that the astrologer has it all wrong. (I will not take the time to list all the scientific evidence that has proven astrology wrong, but believe me it is overwhelming.)

Other Clues From the Bible

We have seen that God made the stars to be for signs and seasons. Psalms 8:3 also shows that it was God and not chance that set them in their specific places:

> *When I consider thy heavens, the work of thy fingers, the moon and the stars, which thou host ordained* [literally set or appointed] (KJV).

The Bible itself reveals that the constellations in the heavens have their origin in antiquity. In the book of Job, which is the oldest penned book in the Bible (written around 1520 B.C.—more than 3500 years ago), we find several references to some principal constellations. The following passages from Job state:

> *Which maketh Arcturus, Orion, and Pleiades, and the chambers of the south.* [Pleiades is Taurus and the Chambers of the South is Scorpio] (Job 9:9 KJV).

> *By his spirit he hath garnished the heavens; his hand hath formed the crooked serpent* [Hydra] (Job 26:13 KJV).

> *Canst thou bind the sweet influence of Pleiades, or loose the bands of Orion?*(Job 38:31 KJV)

> *Canst thou bring for Mazzaroth in his season? Or canst thou guide Arcturus with his sons?* (Job 38:32 KJV)

Mazzaroth is the Hebrew name for the Zodiac and Arcturus is in the constellation *Bootes*, the shepherd harvester.

Both the Bible and history prove the widespread knowledge of the constellations among the people of ancient times. In fact, there is internal evidence in the zodiac found in Denderah, Egypt, that it was copied from a zodiac originally designed around 5,000 years ago based on the position of the planetary bodies. Arastus, the poet quoted by Paul in Acts 17:28, wrote *Phainomena the Phenomenons* about 279 B.C. His writings were based on work done by Eudoxos (403-350 B.C.) Arastus recorded and explained all the signs as they were known to the Greeks of his day.

An interesting fact in his work emerges to help prove our argument that the true source of the signs is divine. The constellations, which he described, were not all visible from the city of Tarsus. As an example, the Southern Cross was included in his work but had not been visible in that part of the world for over 2,000 years! In 1502, Amerigo Vespucci sailed toward the Cape of Good Hope and confirmed the existence of the Southern Cross as being more than mere legend.

When I studied the history of the Zodiac, I was amazed that every ancient civilization in the world had relatively the same constellations and star names. All the records concur even though they were maintained in different cultures around the world. The records have an underlying harmony that is easily understood when one possesses the keys that unlock the code.

Chapter Two

The Keys to Unlock the Code

The keys that unlock the code of how to read the constellations is found in a few scriptures in the Bible. One of the best clues is found in a familiar passage in the book of Psalms 19.

> *The heavens declare the glory of God; and the firmament sheweth his handiwork, Day unto day uttereth speech, and night unto night sheweth Knowledge. There is no speech nor language, where their voice is not heard, Their line is gone out through all the earth, and their words to the end of the world* (Psalms 19:1-4).

It says the heavens declare the glory of God. The word "declare" in Hebrew is *Saphar* and means "to recount or inscribe as a writer." Verse two states: "night unto night sheweth knowledge." The word "sheweth" in Hebrew is *chava* and means "to declare or reveal." From this we can see that we are supposed to be able to gain knowledge from the heavens at night, because knowledge is declared, shown, and revealed at night, and this knowledge is the glory of God (we will discuss this further). Psalms 19:3 states: "There is not speech or language where their voice is not heard." This shows that no matter what language a person may speak, the message of the heavens is heard. Verse four will help one to understand this better:

> *Their line is gone out through all the earth, and their words to the end of the world* (Psalms 19:4).

The word "line" in Hebrew is *kav* and is used in Isaiah 28:

> *Whom shall he teach knowledge? and whom shall he make to understand doctrine? Them that are weaned from the milk, and drawn from the breasts* (v. 9 KJV).
>
> *But the word of the LORD was unto them precept upon precept, precept upon precept; line upon line, line upon line: here a little and there a little; that they might go, and fall backward, and be broken and snared, and taken* (v. 13 KJV).

The word *kav* is used in the Bible for measuring lines of judgment and for setting bounds to creation (Job 38:5), and for the gradual giving of the Word of God, which is in Isaiah 28 above. So, the first part of Psalms

19:4 shows that there is a gradual giving of knowledge (here a little, there a little) that has gone out to all the earth. (This is the method with which God chooses to teach people.) Let's look at Psalms 19:4 again.

Their line is gone out through all the earth, and their words to the end of the world.

Notice the last half says "and their words to the end of the world." According to astronomer and author Ben Mayer, the word "astrology" comes from two words *astro* meaning star and *-ology* originally hails from *logia* meaning "words." The biggest secret of all is that the stars have words! This is the second part of the three-part code needed to unlock the message of the stars. (Remember the first part is to know God hung banners/signs in the heavens in the very beginning.) What words do the stars have? The answer to this is found in the two following scriptures.

God Numbered and Named the Stars

He telleth the number of the stars; he calleth them all by their names (Psalms 147:4 KJV).

Lift your eyes and look to the heavens: Who created all these? He who brings out the starry host one by one, and calls them each by name. Because of his great power and mighty strength, not one of them is missing (Isaiah 40:26 KJV).

God named the stars and passed the revelation of the names of the stars to ancient man. An interesting thing about God is that when he names someone or something, there is always a meaning behind the name. For example, God changed Abram's name to Abraham, which means "the father of nations." This pattern is repeated hundreds of times in the Bible. This is the third part of the code needed to understand this system of symbols in the heavens. Look for the meaning behind the ancient names of the stars.

The constellations also help complete the story. The word "constellation" in all Germanic languages except English means "star picture." Originally, the message of the stars was given and handed down from generation to generation. Don't try to obtain pictures from the arrangement of the stars. The names of the stars in order of brightness were mnemonics (memory aids) to remind them of the picture stories. (Some of the constellations do look much like what the ancient Zodiac portrays, however.)

There is one more scripture we need to review in Psalms 50:6:

> *And the heavens proclaim his righteousness for God himself is judge. Selah.*

The heavens declare God's glory and righteousness. We have learned that the heavens reveal knowledge throughout all the earth and words to the end of the world. What you are about to study is a mystery that has been understood by very few people and yet the keys to understanding it have been in the Bible all along.

Chapter Three

The Ancient Zodiac

Among the many constellations, or groups of stars, there are 12 that lie along the ecliptic, the apparent mean path of the sun in the sky. We call that path the Zodiac. (The 12 constellations that lie on that path also give their names to the "signs" of the Zodiac in astrology.)

The names of the constellations are essentially the same in all languages and go back to the tower of Babel. The Babylonians introduced a corruption from the earlier use of these signs. Ancient Persian and Arabian traditions credit the invention of astronomy to Adam, Seth, and Enoch. The name "Zodiac," as we saw earlier, comes from the Hebrew root *zodi*, meaning "the way". The words "the way" were used in naming the Christian church in the first century in Acts 19:9 and 23, 22:24, 24:14 and 24:27. It has also been called the way of salvation, the way of God. Look how John the Baptist used "the way":

As it is written in the book of the words of

> *Esaias the prophet, saying, "The voice of one crying in the wilderness, Prepare ye the way of the Lord, make his paths straight"* (Luke 3:4 KJV).

We find that all these lead us to one person as John the Baptist prophesied and announced:

> *The next day John seeth Jesus coming unto him and saith, "Behold, the Lamb of God which taketh away the sin of the world"* (John 1:29 KJV).

Jesus said the following words about Himself:

> *Jesus saith unto him, "I am the way, the truth, and the life: no man cometh unto the Father, but by me"* (John 14:6 KJV).

The Zodiac tells of a way, not only the way of the sun, but also the way of the Son of God. When we explore the ancient names of the stars and constellations from a biblical standpoint, we find that they lay out God's plan of redemption. This plan must involve the promised Messiah, Jesus Christ, since He is so deeply involved in God's plan. Amazingly, the stars and the Bible tell the same story.

There are 48 ancient constellations that form a huge circle in the sky (see the diagram in the back of the book). There are 12 major signs, each assigned 30° of the 360° that are in the Zodiac. The circle of the Zodiac is also divided into smaller arcs of ten degrees called *decans* (from a Hebrew word meaning division—remember the word *Kav* on p. 9). So we find that each major sign also has three decan signs that go with it for a total of 48.

How To Begin Reading This Circular Story

The clue that has been left for us to help find the beginning of the heavenly story was found in the mysterious Sphinx. Legend says that the Sphinx guards some hidden knowledge. The sphinx is a composite of two figures: the head of a woman and the body of a lion. The word *sphinx* itself means "to bind closely together." A scholar named Frances Rolleston discovered that there was a representation of the Sphinx placed just below and between the figures of Virgo and Leo on the Zodiac chart in the temple at Enesh, Egypt. Therefore, the Sphinx serves to show us to begin with the head of the woman (Virgo) and end with the lion (Leo).

We are now fully informed on how to read the Zodiac and where to begin and end. We will look at the ancient names of the signs and stars and put together its message, building it line upon line:

> *Their line is gone out through all the earth, and their words to the end of the world* (Psalms 19:4).

Virgo (The Virgin)

Coma (The Desired Son) Centaurus (The Despised)
Bootes (The Coming Shepherd)

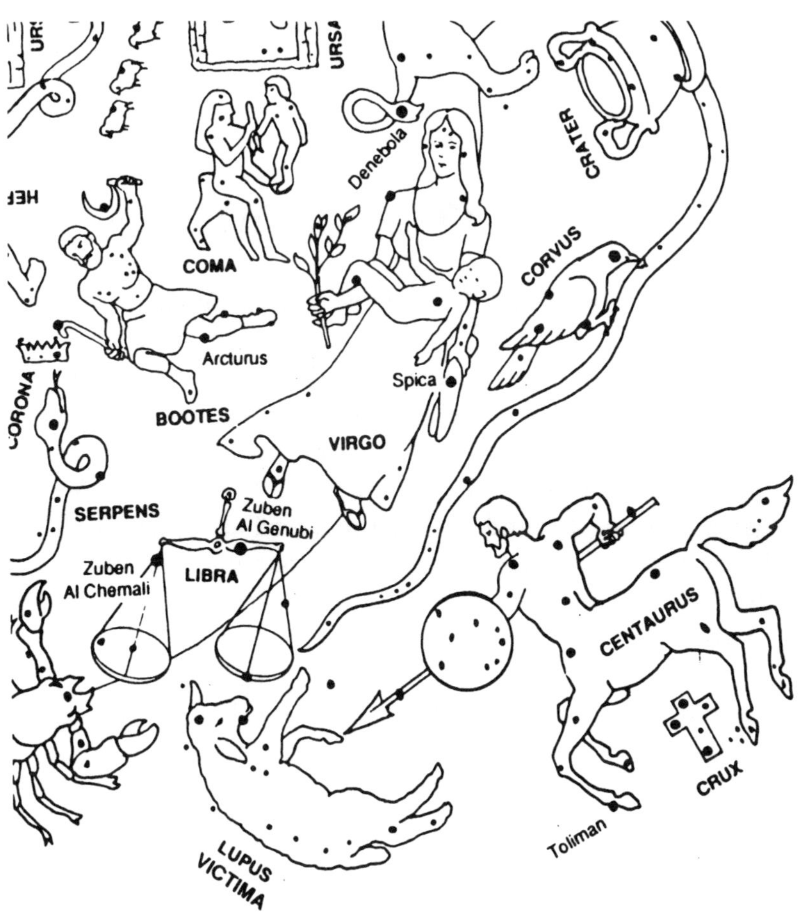

Chapter Four

Virgo (The Virgin)

Virgo is the figure of a woman holding an ear or two of corn in her left hand and a branch in her right hand. All civilizations have seen her this way with some showing her also holding a baby. Virgo begins the first one-third of the heavenly story, with Virgo and Sagittarius facing one another like bookends. (An amazing thing I found is that the 12 tribes of Israel all had standards, or flags, with a corresponding sign of the Zodiac imprinted on them. (See the list on page 122.) Virgo is associated with the tribe of Zebulon,)

The Latin name *Virgo* means "a virgin" and *Virga*, means "a branch." The Latin vulgate uses both words referring to Christ—"virgin born" in Matthew 1:23 and as "the Branch" in Isaiah 11:1:

> *And there shall come forth a rod out of the stem of Jesse, and a Branch shall grow out of his roots* (KJV)*:*

In the more ancient languages, the meanings and

parallels are evident. The Hebrews called her *Bethula*, meaning "the virgin," and that is the common word for virgin in the Old Testament. The Greeks called her *Parthenos*, which is the word used for virgin in the New Testament, particularly in Matthew 1:23:

> *Behold, a virgin* [parthenos] *shall be with child, and shall bring forth a son, and they shall call his name Immanuel, which being interpreted is God with us* (KJV).

The Arabs called her *Adarah*, "the pure virgin," or *Sunbul*, meaning "an ear of corn," which correctly places the emphasis on the seed which will become more evident when we look at the names of the stars. In Egypt, she was named *Aspolio*, which means "the seed." The ancient Chinese, as early as 5000 B.C., called her "the barren woman." In Coptic, she was *Aspolia*, "the place of the desired branch." The Babylonians called Virgo "The Great Mother," and the Assyrians called her *Mylitt* or *Mylitta*— "she who brings forth." In ancient Gaul, an altar was built and dedicated to her around 100 B.C. and had the inscription "to the virgin who is to bring forth." Thus, it is seen that Virgo, although a virgin, is to have a child and the emphasis will be seen to be on the child after we look at the star names.

Star Names of Virgo

In Virgo's left hand is a bright star named *Spica*, which in Latin means "an ear or seed of corn." The

Hebrews called this star *Zerah*, which means "the seed' and is the same exact word used in Genesis 3:14-15.

> *And the LORD God said unto the serpent, Because thou has done this, thou art cursed above all cattle, and above every beast of the field; upon thy belly shalt thou go, and dust shalt thou eat all the days of thy life: And I will put enmity between thee and the woman, and between thy seed and her seed* [Zerah], *it shall bruise thy head, and thou shalt bruise his heel* (KJV).

This is also the first prophecy given in the Bible that shows someone who would be the seed of the woman would come to defeat the serpent (Satan). The virgin birth of the Messiah is hidden in this passage. It is the man and not the woman who carries the seed. In Greek, the word for seed is *sperma*, and the man and not the woman has the seed (sperma). The oldest known Hebrew name for this star, however, is *tsemech*, which means "the branch" and is seen on the oldest star charts. There are 20 Hebrew words for branch, but *tsemech* is used exclusively for the Messiah and is found only five times in Scripture:

> *Hear now, 0 Joshua the high priest, thou, and thy fellows that sit before thee; for they are men wondered at: for, behold, I will bring forth my servant the Branch* (Zechariah 3:8 KJV).

And speak unto him saying, Thus speaketh the LORD of hosts, saying, Behold the man whose name is the Branch (Zechariah 6:12 KJV).

Behold, the days come, saith the LORD, that I will raise unto David a righteous Branch, and a King shall reign and prosper, and shall execute judgment and justice in the earth. In his days Judah shall be saved, and Israel shall dwell safely: and this is his name whereby he shall be called, The Lord Our Righteousness (Jeremiah 23:5-6 KJV). (See also similar scripture in Jeremiah 33:15.)

In that day shall the branch of the LORD be beautiful and glorious...(Isaiah 4:2 KJV).

The above scriptures show that the branch will be a servant, righteous, a king, the Lord, beautiful, and glorious. The second brightest star in this constellation is *Zavijaveh*, located at the tip of the right shoulder, and means "gloriously beautiful," which agrees with Isaiah 4:2 above. In the right arm, there is a star the Arabians called *Al Murredin*, which means "who shall come down or have dominion." The Chaldeans called it *Vindemiatrix*, which means "the Son or Branch who cometh." The Greeks called it *Prometheus*—"the deliverer or branch (bough) who cometh."

The first sign reveals that someone known as the seed and the branch will come down to earth and be born of a virgin. He comes as a deliverer and to have dominion and in some way will be gloriously beautiful. Thus, Virgo's message parallels the Gospel story.

Coma (The Desired Son)

The first decan constellation of Virgo that declares the gospel in the heavens is *Coma*, a virgin woman seated, holding and feeding a child. Some charts actually show this virgin breastfeeding her child. *Coma* is an ancient Hebrew name and means "the desired" or "the longed for." In the book of Haggai, the same word is used when speaking of the longed for Messiah:

> *And I will shake all nations, and the desire of all nations shall come* (Haggai 2:7).

Albumazer, a famous eighth century Arabian astronomer, wrote: "There arises in the first decan, as the Persians, Chaldeans, and Egyptians teach, a young woman whose Persian name denotes a pure virgin sitting on a throne, nourishing an infant boy having a Hebrew name, by some nations called *Ihesu*, with the signification *Ieza*, which in Greek is called *Christos.*" Bear in mind that this Arabian astronomer was not a Christian!

Satan knew he had to change this constellation because it was obviously a Messianic prophecy and confirmed Jesus as the Messiah. Satan arranged history so that we find in the place of Coma, a wig named *Coma Bernicae*, "the hair of Bernice." Most modern star charts do not list Coma, but list Coma Bernice since about 1590 A.D. It was probably in Coma that a new "guest" star appeared, which was the star of Bethlehem that was seen by the wise men. A well known prophecy in the East was that a new star would appear in this sign when He whom it foretold was to be born! This prophecy is traditionally attributed to the prophet Daniel. Many people have written that the wise men were Jews from Babylon and followed the teachings and prophecies of Daniel. Daniel was put in charge of all the wise men in Babylon over 500 years before Jesus was born.

> *Then the king placed Daniel in a high position and lavished many gifts on him. He made him ruler over the entire province of Babylon and placed him in charge of all its wise men* (Daniel 2:48).

Coma reveals that the seed of the woman was to be the "child born and the son given (Isaiah 9:6). When the wise men (Magi) saw the new star, they came looking for the new born child:

> *After Jesus was born in Bethlehem in Judea, during the time of King Herod, Magi from the east came to Jerusalem and asked, "Where is the one who has been born king of the Jews? We saw his star in the east and have come to worship him"* (Matthew 2:12).

Notice that the Magi asked, "Where is he who has been born king?" They said "born" because this constellation shows it was time for the child to be nourished and the prophecy indicated a new star would appear when He whom it foretold was to be born! No doubt the wise men knew to come to Jerusalem because the Messiah was to come from Israel. Notice they came to worship Him. Let's keep reading the story and look for other facts:

> *When he had called together all the people's chief priests and teachers of the law, he asked them where the Christ was to be born. "In Bethlehem in Judea," they replied, "for this is what the prophet has written: 'But you, Bethlehem, in the land of Judah, are by no means least among the rulers of Judah; for out of you will come a ruler who will be the shepherd of my people Israel.'" Then Herod called the Magi secretly and found out from them the exact time the star had appeared. He sent them to Bethlehem and said, "Go and make a careful search for the child. As soon as you find him, report to me, so that I too may go and worship him"* (Matthew 2:4-8).

The wise men had to look at another prophecy to discover exactly where the Christ was to be born, and it was found to be in Bethlehem. Who did the wise men find? Jesus Christ who had been born of the virgin Mary. The wise men knew the star teaching 2,000 years ago! From the knowledge they possessed, they found Jesus and worshipped Him. As the popular saying goes: Wise men still seek Him.

Star Names of Coma

The star names reinforce the overall message of Virgo and her decans. The star named *Subilah* means "who bears" in Hebrew, and *Adrenosa* means "The virgin who carries" in Arabic. We now see that a virgin would carry (in pregnancy) and bear a child named "the seed" and "the branch." In fact, a star named *Hazanethon* meaning "the branch" is located over the child the virgin holds. Thus, this sign ties us back to the seed and branch of Virgo. Most of the signs will have a star that is named "the seed" and/or "the branch" to show when we are speaking of the one born of a virgin in Virgo. This "desired son" was to be more than an infant born miraculously by a virgin. He was to have a dual nature being both divine and human in one body as we shall see in the next decan of Virgo—Centaurus.

Centaurus (The Despised)

The second decan of Virgo is *Centaurus*. This constellation along with the Southern Cross displays itself brilliantly in the heavens, although it is not easily seen in the northern latitudes (due to the procession of the equinoxes). It is seen as half-man in its upper body and half-horse in its lower body. It has been seen this way from antiquity, with the man part holding a spear in the right hand and a shield in the left. Centaurs, in legend, were mighty warriors, but were despised by men and the gods. The Hebrew name for it was *Bezeh*, which means "the despised." It is the same word used in Isaiah 53:3 describing the Messiah Jesus:

He is despised and rejected of men; a man of sorrows, and acquainted with grief and we hid as it were our faces from him; he was despised, and we esteemed him not (Isaiah 53:3).

Another name for it in Hebrew, amazingly, is *Asmeath* and means "a sin offering." I ask you, who is the despised sin offering of Isaiah 53?

All we like sheep have gone astray; we have turned every one to his own way; and the LORD hath laid on him the iniquity of us all (Isaiah 53:6 KJV).

Yet it pleased the LORD to bruise him; he hath put him to grief when thou shalt make his soul an offering for sin (Isaiah 53:10 KJV).

Jesus Christ is the despised sin offering and has a dual nature, being both God and man, as Centaurus depicts.

Names of the Stars

The brightest star in Centaurus is *Alpha Centauri,* and it is the closest star to our solar system, being four and one-half light years away. The ancient name for this star is *Toliman* (seen in the foreleg) and means "the heretofore and the hereafter." This reveals the One who said He was the Alpha and Omega in Revelation 1:8, and shows His existence from all eternity. Another star named *Proxima* is Latin for "The Pierced." Let's read the prophecy about the Messiah in Zechariah 12:10:

> *And I will pour upon the house of David, and upon the inhabitants of Jerusalem, the spirit of grace and of supplications: and they shall look upon me whom they have pierced, and they shall mourn for him, as one mourneth for his only son, and shall be in bitterness for him, as one that is in bitterness for his firstborn* (KJV).

The Greeks named Centaurus *Chiron*, also meaning "the pierced," and in mythology he was famed for his skill in hunting, medicine, music, athletics, and prophecy. He also was known as a great teacher and taught the heroes of Greece. He was immortal, but willingly agreed to die after being struck by a poisoned arrow that was intended for someone else. He transferred his immortality to Prometheus. In this legend, the prophetic message about One who would come and willingly die so others might live is told in a corrupted form. I have stated before that Satan has worked over the years to corrupt the original message of the stars and constellations in order to hide this grand revelation.

The Greeks had a second name for this sign, *Pholas,* meaning "the mediator." This speaks of the one "who is the mediator between God and men, the man Jesus Christ" (Timothy 2:5).

There is one more decan in Virgo that will complete this first part of the heavenly revelation, and it is a constellation named *Bootes*.

Bootes (The Coming Shepherd)

Most ancient Zodiacs depict *Bootes* as a herdsman or shepherd. He is pictured bearing a shepherd's crook in his right hand and a sickle in his uplifted left hand. The Greeks called him Bootes, which is taken from the Hebrew root *Bo* meaning "to come." Job mentions a bright star in Bootes named *Arcturus* and may have referred to the whole constellation by this name in Job 9:9; 38:32. Jesus said He would come again in John 14:3:

> *And if I go and prepare a place for you, I will come again, and receive you unto myself' that where I am, there ye may be also (*KJV).

We know Jesus was born of a virgin in Bethlehem, pierced on a cross for our sins, rose from the dead, and left saying He was coming back again. So far, the heavenly revelation agrees with the written revelation (the Bible). What is amazing about all this is that these heavenly prophetic teachings preceded the written Scriptures by thousands of years!

Star Names of Bootes

The brightest star is *Arcturus* and also means "he comes." The theme of the shepherd is brought out with the star at the top of the shepherd's crook, *Al Kalurops,* meaning "the shepherd's crook." Another star, *Mizar*, means "guarding" or "guardian" and was known earlier as *Mirac*, "the coming forth" (like an arrow).

The second brightest star, *Nekkar*, means "The

Pierced" and confirms the fact that the shepherd would be pierced:

> *And 1 will pour out on the house of David and the inhabitants of Jerusalem a spirit of grace and supplication. They will look on me, the one they have pierced* (Zechariah 12:10).

Another star identifies this shepherd, *Merge*, which means "who bruises":

> *And I will put enmity between thee and the woman, and between thy seed and her seed; it shall bruise thy head, and thou shalt bruise his heel* (Genesis 3:15 KJV).

Jesus was to bruise the serpent's head and the serpent would bruise his heel. These are terms that mean there would be a fight, Satan would be defeated, and the seed of the woman would suffer temporary harm. *Murphride* is another star and means "to separate" (like separating sheep from goats). This perfectly matches what Jesus said He would do when He comes back:

> *When the Son of man shall come in his glory, and all the holy angels with him, then shall he sit upon the throne of his glory: And before him shall be gathered all nations: and he shall separate them one from another, as a shepherd divideth his sheep from the goats* (Matthew 25: 31-32 KJV).

I could write a book of 200 pages naming all the different parallels that are found in every different civilization in the world. However, it is my intention from this point forward to remain brief and to the point. The most important thing is that you understand the true ancient message of the stars and that this message agrees with the Bible, which also points us to salvation through Jesus Christ.

NOTE:

If you are in a hurry to read this book, you can read Virgo, Libra, and Scorpio, then skip to Cancer and Leo. This will give you a good understanding of the message in the heavens. It is also my suggestion that if you intend to teach this material in one session, then teach it in this same sequence.

Libra (The Scales)

Crux (The Southern Cross) Victima (The Victim)

Corona (The Crown)

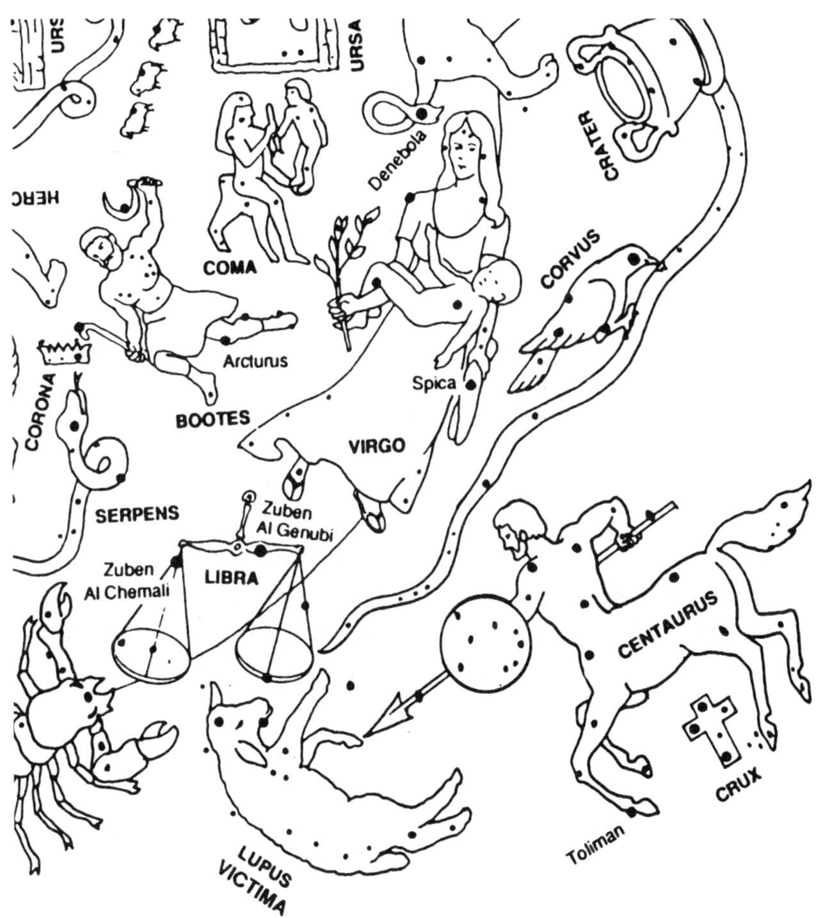

Chapter Five

Libra (The Scales)

The next main constellation in the heavens is a sign named *Libra* that continues where Virgo left off. Virgo showed that "the seed" and "the branch" would come down born of a virgin and be pierced through as a despised sin offering. Libra shows the price which the Savior would pay for the salvation and redemption of mankind. Libra was known in Hebrew as *Mozanaim*, which means "the pair of scales weighing." The Arabians named it *Alzubena*, meaning "the purchase, redemption, or gain." Scales were almost always involved in making purchases in ancient times and are still used in some situations. Libra, therefore, shows a purchase is to be made.

Star Names of Libra

The star names help us know the true message of this sign. The first and brightest star is located on the raised side of the scales and is named *Zuben Al Genubi,* meaning "the price which is deficient." This speaks to the fact that mankind has fallen short of the price that would gain redemption.

> *As it is written: "There is no one righteous, not even one"* (Romans 3:10).

> *For all have sinned and fallen short of the glory of God* (Romans 3:23).

This also reminds me of another time in the book of Daniel when God judged a king and said the following:

> *Tekel: You have been weighed on the scales and found wanting* [deficient] (Daniel 5:27).

The second brightest star located on the lower side of the scales is *Zuben Al Chemali*, which means "the price which covers" or "is sufficient." The only other star is *Zuben Akrabi*, which means "the price of the conflict." What would be the price of the conflict and the price that would cover? The price would be the life of the Messiah. John the Baptist said, "Behold the Lamb of God which taketh away the sins of the world."

Crux (The Southern Cross)

The first decan of Libra is *Crux*, which has always been seen as a cross. As an astronomer, it seems strange to me that this is the only cross in the heavens when there are many other possible combinations of stars that could form crosses. In fact, there are a few that would form more perfect crosses. This constellation was visible to people in the northern hemisphere until it disappeared from view about the time Jesus fulfilled this prophetic sign. Dante, a poet and astronomer of the 12th century, authored the *Divine Comedy*, and in it supposed himself in Jerusalem at the beginning. He mentions he would have seen "'four stars never beheld but by the early race of man." Amerigo Vespucci, on his third Atlantic voyage to the Cape, saw the Southern Cross and said that "he now looked on the four stars never seen until then by any but the first human race."

The ancient name for Crux is *Adom* and means "the cutting off." This sign shows how the Messiah would pay the price for our sins.

The following was prophesied over 500 years before Jesus was born in the book of Daniel the prophet:

> *And after threescore and two weeks shall Messiah be cut off, but not for himself* (Daniel 9:26 KJV).

The word for cut off in Hebrew means "to be executed or slain." The Messiah was to be slain, but how? Daniel does not say, but the heavenly revelation shows he would be cut off on a cross. God knows the end from the beginning. The last letter in the Hebrew alphabet is *tau*, and was originally in the form of a cross. It has the meaning of a boundary mark, a limit, or finish. The prophetical significance of this sign is summed up in the words of Jesus, spoken while hanging on the cross in John 19:30:

> *When he had received the drink, Jesus said "it is*

> *finished" With that, he bowed his head and gave up his spirit.*

The symbol of the cross from early times has been considered a symbol that represents life. Eternal life was purchased for us by the finished work of Jesus Christ, the seed of the woman, the branch, who was born of a virgin.

None of the star names here have been preserved and have probably been lost because the stars of this constellation were not visible for thousands of years. The next sign brings out even more truth concerning Jesus' death.

Victima (The Victim)

In this constellation, we see an animal that has been slain by the spear of Centaurus. This constellation is known by many as *Lupus*, which is Latin for "the wolf." Another name in Latin that bears out the truth of this sign is *Victima*, meaning "the victim," although this name is not the original. The ancient Hebrew name for this sign is *Asedah*, meaning "to be slain." The Arabs called this sign *Asedaton*, which also means "to be slain." Victima has been slain by the spear of Centaurus, demonstrating that the Messiah would willingly sacrifice Himself on the cross:

> *No man taketh it (my life) from me, but I lay it down of myself. I have power to lay it down, and I have power to take it again. This com-*

> *mandment have I received of my Father* (John 10:18 KJV).

> *For then must he often have suffered since the foundation of the world: but now once in the end of the world hath he appeared to put away sin by the sacrifice of himself* (Hebrews 9:26 KJV).

Ulugh Beigh, a Tartar prince and astronomer of the 15th century, working with ancient Arabic astronomical records, drew an atlas with 1,019 stars in their positions in 1437. He wrote that in the earliest Arabian figures, this victim was seen as *Sura,* "the lamb." This also corresponds with the ancient Denderah and Coptic records. Therefore, this sign, which speaks of a lamb slain, is depicted as a lamb. Let's look at the written evidence:

> *He was oppressed, and he was afflicted, yet he opened not his mouth: he is brought as a lamb to the slaughter, and as a sheep before her shearers is dumb, so he openeth not his mouth* (Isaiah 53:7 KJV).

> *And all that dwell upon the earth shall worship him, whose names are not written in the book of life of the lamb slain from the foundation of the world* (Revelation 13:8 KJV).

None of the names of the stars in this sign have been preserved for us. The next sign leads us to a message of victory. It does not end with the cross, but a crown:

Corona (The Crown)

The last decan of Libra is *Corona*, or *Corona Borealis,* "The Crown," or "The Northern Crown." As an astronomer, I enjoy looking into the heavens and have noticed that this sign looks like its name. It forms an arc or semi-circle and is overhead in the early summer sky. In the Bible, after Jesus died, He was crowned! This sign teaches us the same truth:

> *But we see Jesus, who was made a little lower than the angels for the suffering of death, crowned with glory and honor; that he by the grace of God should taste death for every man* (Hebrews 2:9 KJV).

The ancient name for this constellation is *Atatah*, meaning "a kingly or royal crown." This is a crown for the one who would pay the price for our sins and be slain on a cross. This crown is for the King of kings and the Lord of lords!

Names of the Stars

The only star name we have is for the brightest star, *Ai Phecca*, meaning "the shining." Jesus was spoken of as a "light which shineth in darkness" (John 1:5). Remember in Libra, there was a star named *Zuben Akrabi*—"the price of the conflict." This star introduces the fact that there is a conflict and the next sign, *Scorpio*, introduces the enemy of the conflict.

Scorpio (The Scorpion)

Serpens (The Serpent) Orphiuchus (The Serpent Held)
Hercules (The Branch Kneeling)

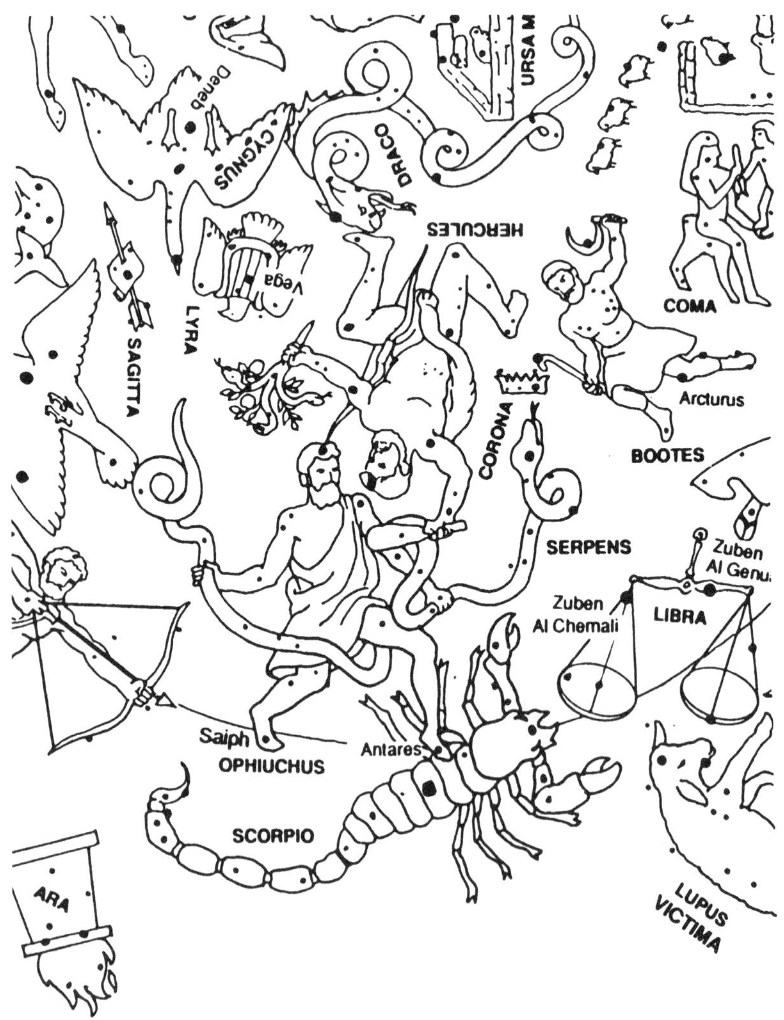

Chapter Six

Scorpio (The Scorpion)

The third scene in the prophetic story of the heavens is *Scorpio*. Of all the constellations in the heavens, this is one of the best to observe visually. This sign depicts a large scorpion trying to sting the heel of the mighty man *Ophiuchus*, who is wrestling with a snake named *Serpens*. Notice the foot of the mighty man is crushing the scorpion. The Hebrews called Scorpio *Arab,* which has a double meaning. It means "scorpion" and also means "conflict" or "war." In Coptic, it was known as *Isdis*, meaning "the attack of the enemy." The Arabic name is *Al Akrab*, which means "wounding him who cometh." Here we see the fulfillment of Genesis 3:15:

> *And I will put enmity between thee and the woman, and between thy seed and her seed; it shall bruise thy head, and thou shalt bruise his heel* (KJV).

In the constellation *Orphiuchus*, "the mighty man,"

there are even more prophetic parallels. In the Bible, the enemy of mankind was spoken of in a figurative sense as being a scorpion, a serpent (or snake), and a dragon among other things.

The Names of the Stars

The brightest star in Scorpio is *Antares,* and to the naked eye, is similar in its appearance to the planet Mars (because it glows red). Antares, in Arabic, means, "the wounding." Some give its meaning as the "rival of *Ares* (Mars). Mars is called the planet of war and this sign means "conflict" or "war." The star in the tail is named *Lesath*, which is Hebrew for "the perverse." This sign shows the conflict between the seed of the woman, (Jesus) and the serpent, scorpion, or dragon enemy in Genesis 3:15. We will look at the serpent and the mighty man next and the dragon sign is soon to come.

Serpens (The Serpent) and *Orphiuchus* (The Serpent Held)

The first and second decans of Scorpio are seen as a mighty man named *Orphiuchus*, holding and struggling with a serpent named *Serpens*. The serpent is struggling to reach *Corona*, the crown, but the mighty man is holding him back. The author of this story has made sure that we understand that the serpent does not capture the crown because it has been awarded to the One who purchased us by being slain on a cross in the constellation of Libra. The battle for this crown is for dominion, and it has been won by the Messiah. It is also clear that the scorpion is being crushed under the foot of this mighty man.

The name *Orphiuchus* comes from the Greek and the Arabic name *Afeichus* means "the serpent held."

Star Names of Serpens and Orphiuchus

The star names add to and confirm our story. The brightest star located in the neck of the serpent is *Unuk*, meaning "encompassing." This star is named *Alyah* in Hebrew, which means "the accursed," and confirms that this is the accursed serpent of Genesis 3:14-15. Another star, *Cheleb*, in Arabic means "the serpent enfolding." In *Orphiuchus*, the brightest star is named in Arabic, *Ras-Al-Hagus,* "the head of him who holds." This same star bears another Arabic name, *Ras-Al-Awa*, which means "the head of the desired one." This is the same name of the star in the head of Hercules. Notice how close the head of Hercules is to Orphiuchus. This shows that they really are the same person and, in fact, are the same persons with the desired one of Coma (who is the seed of the virgin, Virgo). Located in the foot, which is uplifted as if injured (or bruised), is a star name *Saiph*, which is Hebrew for "bruised," and is the same word used in Genesis 3:15:

> *And I will put enmity between thee and the woman, and between thy seed and her seed; it shall bruise thy head, and thou shalt bruise his heel* (KJV).

Bear in mind this is the first prophecy in the Bible that shows there will be a conflict that will involve the seed of the woman. This prophecy implies a virgin birth because the man carries the seed, not the woman. This scripture is also perfectly demonstrated in Scorpio and the decan signs presented here.

Another star in this sign is named *Trophas*, and means "treading underfoot." The Bible story and the heavenly story so consistently match that it can be said they both have the same author—the creator of heaven and earth. Remember that the heavenly revelation came thousands of years before the written revelation. It is the scorpion, the serpent, and as we shall see, the dragon that have tried to hide this story from you.

The last two stars in the constellation are named in Hebrew *Carbebus*, "the wounding," and *Mergeros*, "contending." In Greek mythology, Orphiuchus is known as *Aesculapius*, a person who was considered to be a god and man. He was known to be a physician and healer and even reported to have brought the dead back to life. He became worshipped as the god of health and healing. Representations of him picture him with a serpent or its symbol. This Greek myth, although corrupted, still mirrors Jesus Christ, the only person who has fulfilled these signs in all of history. The reason is because it really is His-story. The wise men proved who the stars are speaking about when they found Jesus in Bethlehem! It is so wonderful to see God's eternal calendar of events written in the indelible ink of the stars!

Hercules (The Branch Kneeling)

The third decan of Scorpio is *Hercules*, who the Egyptians named *Bau*, "the one who cometh." He is pictured holding an uplifted club in one hand and a triple-headed snake monster in the branch of an apple tree in the other hand. He is on one knee because his heel has been bruised, and his other foot is crushing the head of Draco, the dragon. The Chaldeans made note of him 4,000 years ago, and the Greeks saw him as a savior. His name in Arabic is *Al Gisgal*, "the strong one," and in Hebrew it is *Marsic*, which means "the wounding." All his great achievements recorded in myth are corruptions of what the Messiah would do, even down to the fact that Hercules spent three days and nights in the belly of a sea monster. After His death, Jesus Christ spent three days and three nights in the heart of the earth.

> *For as Jonas was three days and three nights in the whale's belly; so shall the Son of man be three days and three nights in the heart of the earth* (Matthew 12:40).

In Greek mythology, Hercules was born after Zeus, his father, impregnated a virgin woman. This made Hercules half god and half man! There are more parallels to the Gospel story that won't be covered in this book, but it is clear that Hercules represents Jesus Christ.

The Names of the Stars

The brightest star in Hercules is located in his forehead and is named in Arabic *Ras-Al-Gethi,* "the head of him who bruises." This star has a second name just like Orphiuchus, which in Arabic is named *Ras-Al-Awa,* "the head of the desired." Coma, the first decan of Virgo, first showed us who the desired one was. Now, here he is again and is seen as the same person as Orphiuchus.

The second brightest star in Hercules is named *Kornephorus*, "the branch kneeling." We first saw a person named the branch in Virgo and here he is again. God intentionally puts the same names like "the seed" or "the branch" or "the desired one" to show us when we are speaking of the same person. Another star in Hebrew is *Marsic*, the meaning as we learned earlier is "the wounding." A star in his left arm is named in Hebrew *Ma'asym,* or "the sin offering." Again, who is the sin offering of Isaiah 53? The answer of course is Jesus. There is a star named *Caiam*, which in Hebrew means "punishing." The desired one is seen punishing Draco the dragon.

Sagittarius (The Archer)

Lyra (The Harp) Ara (The Altar of Fire)

Draco (The Dragon)

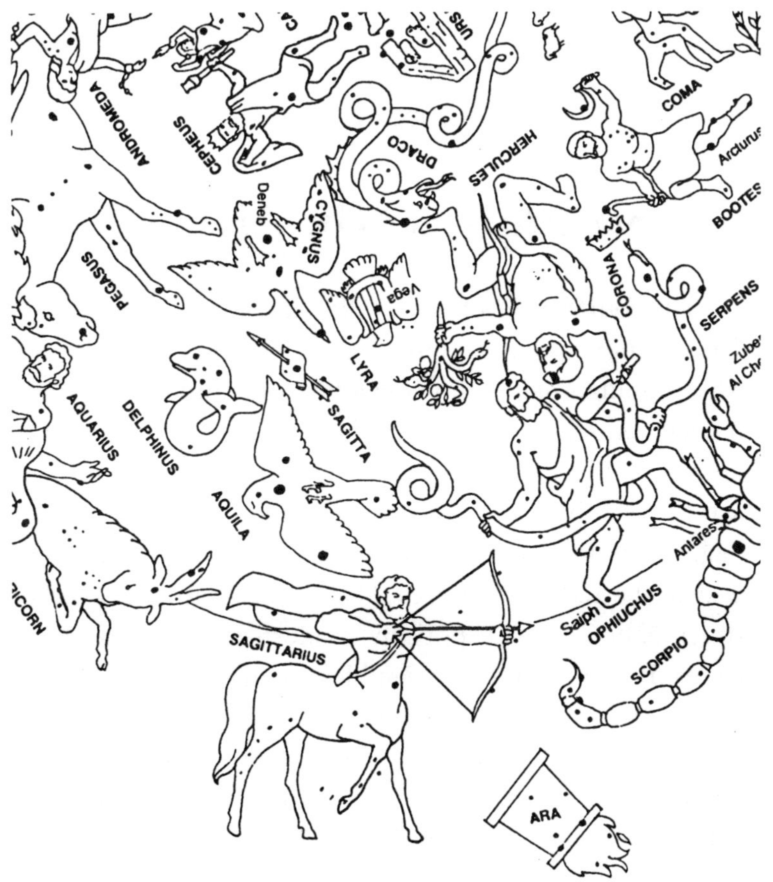

Chapter Seven

Sagittarius (The Archer)

The fourth sign of the Zodiac is called *Sagittarius*, "the archer and conqueror." He appears as a centaur whose human half is drawing a bow and aiming at a star named *Antares* in the constellation *Scorpio*. Antares is known as the heart of the scorpion. He has a quiver of arrows with him and his foreleg is uplifted as if injured. Sagittarius is easily found in the night sky by looking east of the red star Antares. (This constellation is sometimes called "the teapot" by modern astronomers because the star grouping resembles a teapot.)

The Hebrews and the Syrians called this sign *Kesith*, meaning "the bending of a bow" (for shooting). The Arabic name was *Alkaus*, "the arrow," and the Greeks called it *Toxotes*, "the archer." Sagittarius is what the Romans called this sign, and it means "the archer who sends forth the arrow." The Accadians called him *Nunki*, "the prince of the earth."

The Names of the Stars

The brightest star in this sign in Hebrew is named *Naim*, "the gracious one." Two other stars are named in Hebrew: *Nushata*, meaning "the sending forth" and *Terebellum*, meaning "sent forth swiftly." In Greek mythology, Sagittarius was known as *Cheiron*, "the righteous executioner," the chief of the centaurs. He was full of grace, kindness, intelligence, and wisdom. He also was known as a great teacher and revealer of heavenly wisdom being wise in both medicine and art. Sagittarius mirrors the dual nature of the God-man Jesus Christ, and has great wisdom, grace and kindness, just like Jesus does. He has inflicted the first deadly blow against his enemy and will return swiftly as a warrior to finish destroying all the works of Satan. The last star name is *Croton*, a Greek name meaning "the purchaser." Jesus is the one who has purchased us, His lost sheep:

> *And they sang a new song: "You are worthy to take the scroll and to open its seals, because you were slain, and with your blood you purchased men for God from every tribe and language and people and nation"* (Revelation 5:9).

This was shown clearly in Libra. Because of His paying the high price for our souls, He is worthy to be the righteous executioner, executing the righteous judgment on the enemy.

Lyra (The Harp)

The first decan constellation of Sagittarius is *Lyra*, pictured as an eagle rising heavenward with a lyre or harp. This is one of the oldest instruments mentioned in the Bible in the time of Adam (Genesis 4:21). This is the harp that was presented to Orpheus by Apollos in Greek mythology. With this harp, Orpheus could do miraculous things. This sign has to do with praise, singing, and rejoicing.

The Names of the Stars

The brightest star in this sign is *Vega*, which means "he shall be exalted." This reveals to us what the praise and rejoicing of the harp is for. The root meaning of this word is used in Exodus 15:1:

> *Then Moses and the Israelites sang this song to the Lord: "I will sing to the LORD,for he is highly exalted."*

There is joy, praise, and rejoicing in this sign because of the victory of the dual-natured archer. In the same way Moses and the Israelites sang after a great deliverance, there is glad singing at the victory of this righteous archer over the enemy (Scorpio, and as we will see, Draco). This is a victory won for God's people over sin and Satan.

The second brightest star is *Shelyuk*, which is Hebrew for "the fishing eagle." Another star name in Hebrew was *Sulaphat,* which means "springing up" or "ascending." Some old star maps show a harp only, while others showed an eagle in the attitude of triumph. The second way is how the Denderah zodiac showed it. In fact, the Egyptians at Denderah had a figure of an eagle ruling over the serpent and named it *Fent-Kar,* "the serpent ruled." This Zodiac was made around 107 B.C. and is believed to be a copy of one originally designed more than 5,000 years ago, based on the positions of the planetary bodies. "The serpent ruled" is an accurate description of Satan, his present position, and his future fate of eternal punishment, as described in Revelation 20:

> *He seized the dragon, that ancient serpent, who is the devil, or Satan, and bound him for a thousands of years, threw him into the Abyss, and locked and sealed it over him, to keep him from deceiving the nations anymore until the thousand years were ended. After that, he must be set free for a short time* (Revelation 20:2).

> *When the thousand years are over Satan will be released from his prison* (Revelation 20:7).

Here is the final end for Satan and all who are his! The next decan sign will further bring this out:

> *And the devil that deceived them was cast into the lake of fire and brimstone, where the beast and the false prophet are, and shall be tormented day and night for ever and ever* (Revelation 20:10).

Ara (The Altar of Fire)

The third decan of Sagittarius is *Ara,* "the altar" and is shown as an altar upside down, topped with burning fire being poured out. The fire is burning toward regions of outermost darkness. This presents a scene of fiery judgment. The name for this sign in Arabic is *Al Mugamra,* meaning "the completing" or "the finishing." The Greeks had two names for this sign, *Ara* and *Thusiasterion*, which means "the imprecation" (a curse). This reminds us of the curse in Genesis 3:14 that God put on the serpent and also the prophecy of Genesis 3:15, predicting Satan's defeat by "'the seed of the woman." Satan's ultimate end involves eternal fire (see Revelation 20:10 above). The completing or the finishing of the dragon (the devil) puts him in the lake of fire forever. You want to be sure you give your life to God and become a born again Christian (John 3:3), or else the following is an accurate prediction of your future. (Astrologers like to make predictions based on the zodiac. Theirs are based on falsehood, but the following is a sure word.)

> *Then he will say to those on his left "Depart from me, you who are cursed, into the eternal fire prepared for the devil and his angels"* (Matthew 25:41).

To make sure we understand for whom this judgment is meant, God finished this one-third of the story with Draco, the dragon. In fact the second third of the heavenly story (Act Two, I call it) ends with *Cetus*, the sea monster bound and defeated by the mighty Perseus. Act three ends with judgment being poured out on Hydra, the serpent.

Draco (The Dragon)

The last decan of Sagittarius is named *Draco* and is shown as a fierce dragon that is having his head crushed by the mighty Hercules, whom we saw earlier represents the branch of Virgo and the desired one of Coma. Hercules represents the victorious one over the dragon, the serpent, and the scorpion. He is none other than Jesus Christ, the "seed of the woman" who would have his heel bruised in Genesis 3:15, but would crush His enemy's head. The name for this sign in Greek is *Drakon*, and means "trodden down." Dragons, although nonexistent, have always represented evil in every culture. How could a creature never seen by man be so universally used to symbolize evil? The only explanation is that God gave the original revelation to early man in the stars of the heavens and this characterization and nature of the dragon has continued to this day. Remember Psalms 19?

> *Their line is gone out through all the earth, and their words to the end of the world* (Psalms 19:4).

The brightest star in Draco is named in Hebrew *Thuban*, which means "the subtle." About 4,700 years ago, Thuban was the pole star, but the present pole star is located under *Cephus*, "the king's foot." The pole star is considered to be the highest point in all the heavens and shows the authority and dominion has shifted from the dragon to the king! Even the procession of the equinoxes tells the story! (More on this when we look at Cephus.) The Arabic name for this star was *Al Waid,* meaning "he who is about to be destroyed." The second brightest star was named in Hebrew *Rastaban*, "the head of the serpent." The third brightest star is named *Etanino* (Hebrew), meaning "the long serpent." Another star in Hebrew was named *Giansar*, meaning "the punished enemy." The Denderah zodiac shows Sagittarius trampling the serpent under foot. They named the figure *Her-Fent*, "the serpent accursed."

It is amazing how the stories not only reinforce one another, but also harmonize with the greatest book in the world—the Bible. This is easy to believe when you see that both have the same author, God Himself. He is the only one who could write the heavenly story thousands of years before He gave the written revelation. This ends Act One of the prophetic story, now we go on to Act Two.

Capricorn (The Goat Fish)

Sagitta (The Arrow) Aquila (The Pierced One Falling)
Delphinus (The Dolphin)

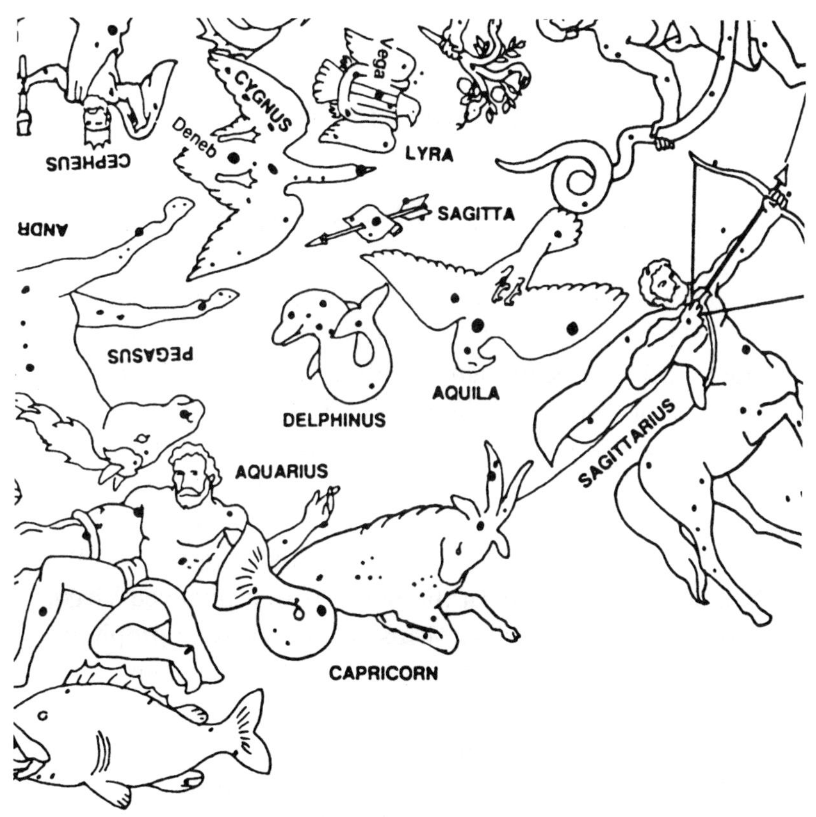

Chapter Eight

Capricorn (The Goat Fish)

Zodiac constellation number five is *Capricorn*, and this sign opens Act Two, which consists of four main signs and 12 decan signs. Capricorn is pictured as the forepart of a goat and the tail of a large healthy fish. The goat is sinking down in death with his right foreleg placed under his body because it has been injured. Again, we have a dual-natured individual that reminds us of the dual-natured Centaurus and Sagittarius. We looked at the first act of the heavens that involved Virgo, Libra, Scorpio, and Sagittarius. These spoke of prophetic truth concerning the person and work of the coming redeemer. Capricornus, Aquarius, Pisces, and Aries will look more at the results of His redeeming work. The Hebrew name for this sign is *Gedi*, meaning "the kid" and "cut off." We have seen that the redeemer would be cut off on a cross, which fulfilled a prophecy in Daniel 9:26:

> *And after threescore and two weeks shall Messiah be cut off, but not for himself.*

Let's look at how it is used in another scripture and bear in mind that all of Isaiah 53 speaks of the Messiah, Jesus Christ:

> *He was taken from prison and from judgment: and who shall declare his generation? for he was cut off out of the land of the living: for the transgression of my people was he stricken* (Isaiah 53:8 KJV).

The Coptic name for this sign is *Hupenius*, "the station of bearing" or "the place of birth." Although it is hard to interpret this sign without Bible knowledge, it is not hard to understand when you know the Bible. Because of the death of the goat, something is to be born. This will be the giving of life to the fish. Let's focus on the goat first. A goat or kid was sacrificed for sin offerings in the Old Testament. These sacrifices were done until the one true sacrifice was accomplished in the death of Jesus, as a final sin offering. Actually, the sacrifice of lambs, goats, etc., were pointing to and giving meaning to the purpose of the death of the Messiah. The goat, as a sacrificial animal, speaks to us of the atonement.

> *And unto the children of Israel thou shalt speak, saying "Take ye a kid of the goats for a sin offering; and a calf and a Lamb, both of the first year, without blemish, for a burnt offering"* (Leviticus 9:3 KJV).

And he brought the people's offering, and took the goat, which was the sin offering for the people, and slew it, and offered it for sin, as the first (Leviticus 9:15 KJV).

The meaning and purpose of this goat in the sky is to be a sin offering, which the star names will soon prove. Another message is being presented in the fish part of this sign. Before we look at its message, let's notice something. All ancient zodiacs have this rather strange combination of goat and fish. This sign, like Draco the dragon, does not exist in nature and yet all ancient civilizations saw this sign the same way! How could they all come up with the same star picture when most of the constellations do not look like what they depict? In other words, you cannot go outside at night and see all the signs in the starry sky looking exactly like they do on the star maps. Only some of them resemble what they are supposed to depict. This goes further to prove that there must have been an original revelation from God that ancient man kept sacred and preserved. History and the Bible show that the Zodiac was changed from its essential purpose during the time of Nimrod at the tower of Babel. At this time, all the people spoke the same language, but God made it where there were many languages among the people and, at this time, they spread out across the earth. Let's look at what happened:

And the whole earth was of one language, and of one speech (Genesis 11:1).

> *And they said, "Go to, let us build us a city and a tower, whose top may reach unto heaven; and let us make a name, lest we be scattered abroad upon the face of the whole earth"* (Genesis 11:4 KJV).

God had commanded them to fill all the earth, and they were not doing what He said. They also were building the tower of Babel to use to worship the stars and planets. This tower was built on seven stages or levels to correspond to the seven planets. God decided to do something about it:

> *Come, let us go down, and there confound their language, that they may not understand one another's speech. So the LORD scattered them from there all over the earth, and they stopped building the city. Therefore is the name of it called Babel; because the LORD did there confound the language of all the earth: and from thence did the LORD scatter them abroad upon the face of all the earth* (Genesis 11: 7~9 KJV).

One ancient Babylonian tablet reads "The building of this illustrious tower offended the gods. In a night they threw down what they had built. They scattered them abroad and made strange their speech. Their progress was impeded. They wept hot tears for Babylon." Genesis 10 has the genealogies of Noah and his sons. There is a special event mentioned that happened after the tower of Babel:

And unto Eber were born two sons: the name of one was Peleg; for in his days was the earth divided; and his brother's name was Joktan (Genesis 10:25 KJV).

In the days of Peleg, the earth was divided from being one continent to many. So, the knowledge of the stars was spread across all the earth. This is the only reasonable explanation I can ascertain to account for all ancient civilizations having essentially the same zodiac and star names. Again, the fish part has some symbolic meaning. Fish in the Bible is associated with people:

But, the LORD liveth, that brought up the children of Israel from the land of the north, and from all the lands whither he had driven them: and I will bring them again into their land that I gave unto their fathers. Behold, I will send forth many fishers, saith the LORD, and they shall fish them (Jeremiah 16:15 KJV).

Jesus said "Follow me and I will make you fishers of men" (Matthew 4:19).

Again, the kingdom of heaven is like unto a net, that was cast into the sea, and gathered of every kind: Which, when it was full, they drew to shore, and sat down, and gathered the good (fish) into vessels, but cast the bad away. So shall it be at the end of the world: the angels

> *shall come forth, and sever the wicked from among the just* (Matthew 13:47-49 KJV).

One of the most popular Christian symbols today is that of the fish. The people of the early church referred to themselves as "The Way," "His Fish," "His Bride," and "His Sheep." The Greek word for fish is *Icythus*, which creates an acrostic for the first letters of the Greek words Jesus Christ—God's Son—Savior. It is amazing to see the same symbolism in the heavens. During the time of the persecutions, the Christians were not sure who to trust, so one would draw what looked like a half-circle in the ground. If the other person was a Christian, he would finish the drawing to look like a fish. Let's look at the star names and other decan constellations in this sign so we can more fully comprehend the meaning of Capricorn.

Star Names of Capricorn

The brightest star in this sign is named in Arabic *Al Gedi* and means "the goat." The second brightest star in Arabic is named *Deneb Al Gedi*, which means "the Lord," or "sacrifice cometh." *Al Dabih* (Arabic) means "the sacrifice slain." So the stars show the goat part is slain and the living fish comes from the death of this goat. The last decan sign of this constellation is *Delphinus*, the dolphin, and shows the fish no longer connected to the goat, but free. Jesus is pictured as dying but bringing forth much fruit because of His death. In the Bible, the people of God are the fruit, the fish, the sheep, and the bride.

Sagitta (The Arrow)

The first decan of Capricornus is *Sagitta*, "the arrow of God's divine judgment." This judgment was due to be inflicted upon all mankind, but instead was inflicted upon the Son of God, who took away the sin of the world. There is a message on paper stuck to the arrow, and it is hard to say what that message is. Let me, however, make some interesting observations concerning the law of Moses known as the *Torah*. The Hebrew verb related to the noun Torah is *Yarah*, which means "to shoot an arrow." The Torah contains 613 laws, which the Bible shows that no man could live up to. Perhaps this paper represents the law of God that has the written judgments against sin. God has shot out the arrow (judgment) of His law. Because no one could keep the law, the law brought a curse and judgment:

> *For as many as are of the works of the law are under the curse: for it is written, Cursed is every one that continueth not in all things which are written in the book of the law to do them* (Galatians 3:10 KJV).

The problem was that no one could live up to God's standard of perfection. The purpose of the law was to show us our need for a redeemer and a savior. If you could not keep the whole law, then you were under the curse. Jesus took the curse upon himself:

> *Christ hath redeemed us from the curse of the*

> *law, being made a curse for us: for it is written, Cursed is every one that hangeth on a tree* (Galatians 3:13 KJV).

The name for this sign in Hebrew was *Scham*, meaning "destroying" and is seen in its intended role in the death of a goat and the death of the eagle, Aquila, which is the next sign. Ancient legend says that it was this arrow that pierced Aquila, the pierced eagle, which is also the next decan sign of Capricornus.

Star Names of Sagitta

The only star name we have is that of the second brightest, *Al Kaus,* "the arrow."

Aquila (The Pierced One Falling)

The second decan of Capricornus is *Aquila*, which is pictured as an eagle that is falling from the sky. Aquila, according to ancient legend, is said to have been pierced by the arrow Sagitta. In fact, some of the ancient zodiacs show the tip of the arrow touching the eagle. This constellation, like Capricornus, is sinking in death to bring forth new life. The Hebrew name for this sign is *Taraed*, which means "the wounded," and also is the name of the third brightest star.

Star Names of Aquila

The brightest star, *Al Tair* means "the wounding" in Arabic. The second brightest star in Arabic is *Al Shain*, "the bright" or "scarlet colored." This word is from a root word that means "red colored." This reminds us of the color of blood. Two other Arabic names are *Al Cair,* which means "the piercing" and *Al Okab*, which means "wounded in the heel." This last meaning, "wounded in the heel," reminds us of two mighty men, Orphicius and Hercules, who have also been wounded (bruised) in the heel. It also reminds us of the prophesy of Genesis 3:15.

The last star is named *Deneb*, which is Hebrew for "the Lord" or "judge cometh." Deneb was also found in Capricornus (in the goat part), which shows they represent the same person. First of all, the main sign is given and then the decan signs are given to help explain the main sign. We have seen Capricornus, half goat and half fish. The goat is sinking in death. Why? Sagitta the arrow explains why and then Aquila comes along to further explain the purpose of the goat and whom it represents. The only thing left is to further explain the fish part of Capricornus.

Delphinus (The Dolphin)

The last decan in Capricornus is *Delphinus*, which is seen as a healthy fish no longer tied to the dying goat, but alive, alone, and free. This dolphin is shown springing up out of death. In the fourth century, this was the symbol used to commemorate Christ's crucifixion and resurrection. This sign not only shows the resurrection of the one "wounded in the heel," but also many people springing to new life because of His death. Romans 6 speaks to this truth:

Know ye not, that so many of us as were bap-

tized into Jesus Christ were baptized into His death? Therefore we are buried with him by baptism into death: that like as Christ was raised up from the dead by the glory of the Father, even so we also should walk in newness of life (Romans 6:3-4 KJV).

Notice how it is put again in Romans 4:

He was delivered over to death for our sins and was raised to life for our justification (Roman 4:25).

The following scripture says it best of all:

I tell you the truth, unless a kernel of wheat falls to the ground and dies, it remains only a single seed. But if it dies, it produces many seeds (John 12:24).

The kernel of wheat has died (Christ) and from His death many seeds (Christians or "little Christs") have come into being. This is the message of this sign and will be further proved to be true by the use of the fish in other places in the Zodiac. In order to enter this mystical body here represented as a fish, Jesus said "You must be born again." He went on further to explain:

Jesus answered, "Verily, verily, I say unto thee, Except a man be born of water and of the Spirit, he cannot enter into the kingdom of God" (John 3:5 KJV).

And finally, to complete His words:

> *And as Moses lifted up the serpent in the wilderness, even so must the Son of man be lifted up:* [on a cross] *That whosoever believeth in him should not perish, but have eternal life* (John 3:14-15 KJV).

In Denderah, Egypt's zodiac, Deiphinus was named in hieroglyphics *Khau*, meaning "a multitude." There will be a multitude of new fish (people) born because of His death.

> *After this I beheld, and lo, a great multitude, which no man could number, of all nations, and kindreds, and peoples, and tongues, stood before the throne, and before the lamb, clothed with white robes, and palms in their hands* (Revelation 7:9 KJV).

Star Names of Delphinus

Two stars here are named in Arabic *Dalaph*, meaning "coming quickly" and *Scalooin*, meaning "swift" (as the flowing of water). The Syrian name and the Chaldean names *Rotaneb* and *Rotaneu* mean "swiftly running" (like running water). The message of water will be brought out in our next constellation, Aquarius, the water pourer.

Aquarius (The Water Pourer)

Piscis Australis (The Southern Fish) Pegasus (The Winged Horse) Cygnus (The Swan Circling)

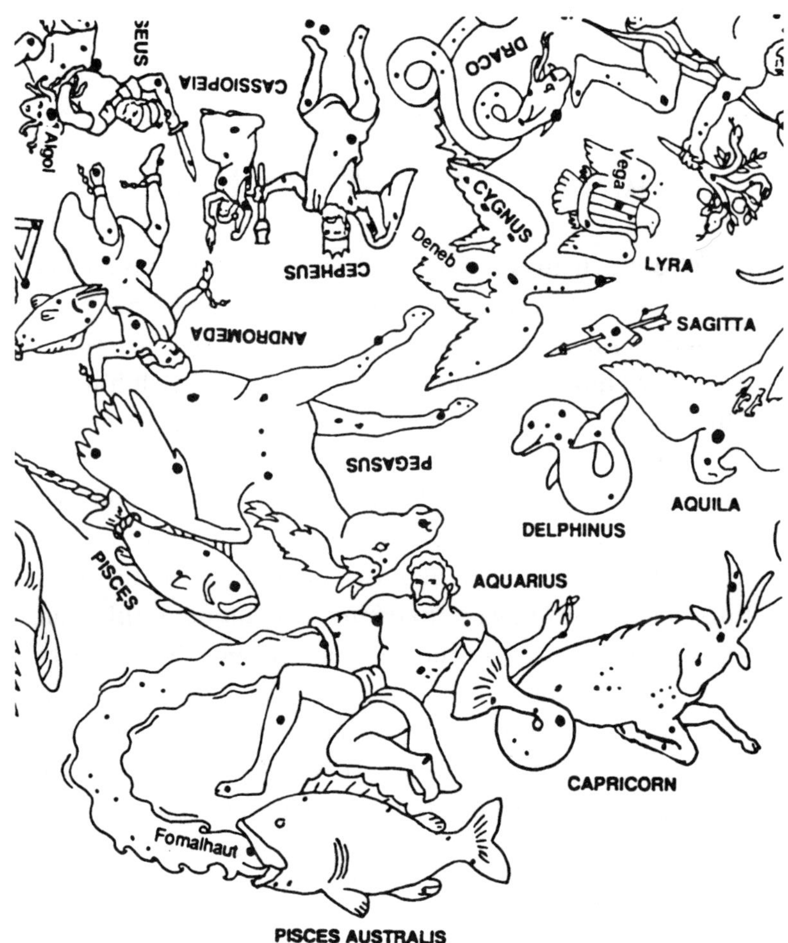

Chapter Nine

Aquarius (The Water Pourer)

The sixth major zodiacal sign in the heavens is *Aquarius*, and he is shown as a man on one knee with his left hand pointed in the direction of the last three decans we have studied (Sagitta, Aquila, and Delphinus). This seems to indicate that the action and message of this sign is related to or the result of what these preceding signs revealed. In his right hand he holds an urn from which he pours a seemingly endless stream of water that runs swiftly like a river into the mouth of a huge fish names *Piscis Austrinus.* The name of this sign in Latin is *Aquarius*, and means "the pouring forth of water." The Hebrew name is *Deli*, "the water urn," and the Arabic and Syriac names have the same meaning. The Coptic name is Hupeitirion, "the place of his coming down as rain." It is no surprise that water is used in the signs of the heavens because water represents so many truths in the Bible:

> *Then shall we know, if we follow on to know the LORD: his going forth is prepared as the*

> *morning: and he shall come unto us as the rain, as the latter and former rain unto the earth* (Hoses 6:3 KJV).

I would also expect that God would make sure he spoke of His plan to pour His spirit out to His people on earth because of the end-time prophecy in the book of the prophet Joel:

> *And it shall comes to pass afterward, that I will pour out my spirit upon all flesh; and your sons and your daughters shall prophesy, your old men shall dream dreams, your young men shall see visions: And also upon the servants and upon the handmaids in those days will I pour out my spirit* (Joel 2:28-29).

It reads "I will pour out of My spirit...." This is the truth presented in this sign.

Jesus commanded His disciples to wait for the outpouring and baptism of the Holy Spirit and called it "the promise of the Father." Luke records in the book of Acts Jesus' words about this outpouring.

> *But you will receive power when the Holy Spirit comes on you; and you will be my witnesses in Jerusalem., and in all Judea and Samaria, and to the ends of the earth* (Acts 1:8).

Star Names of Aquarius

The brightest star in this sign is named in Arabic *Sa'ad Almelik* meaning "the record of the pouring out." A star located in the shoulder has another name, *Saab Al Suud,* which means "the pourer out of the water." Another star named in Hebrew is *Scheat*, meaning "who goeth and returneth." This same name is found in Capricorn and Pegasus. Jesus is the one who came, left the earth, and is returning again. There is a star located in the urn named *Ancha*, "the vessel of pouring out."

Piscis Australis (The Southern Fish)

The first decan of Aquarius is *Piscis Australis,* which is seen as a large fish with a wide open mouth receiving all the water that Aquarius pours out of his great urn. This represents and fulfills the invitation of Jesus to "come unto Me and drink." The fish represents (as we have seen) the mystical group of people who live because of the death of the goat half of Capricornus.

First, we have seen the fish attached to the goat, then the fish was set free from the goat, and now this fish receives the water of life. Jesus said, "Whosoever shall drink of the water that I shall give him shall never thirst." The idea of never thirsting again has to do with eternal life and is represented by the fact that the urn of Aquarius has an endless supply of water. This heavenly water is indeed intended to be a blessing.

Star Names of Piscis Australis

The ancient name of this sign is also the same as the

only star name preserved for us—*Fomalhaut*, Arabic for "the mouth of the fish."

Pegasus (The Winged Horse)

The second decan of Capricornus is *Pegasus*, which is shown as the top half of a winged horse. Again we see a picture of an animal that has never existed in nature before, and we must look for the symbolic message it portrays. Perhaps this is one half of the dual natured one symbolized in Centaurus and Sagittarius. Pegasus in Greek means "coming quickly, joyfully." Let's see what information the star names can give us.

Star Names of Pegasus

The brightest star in Pegasus is named *Markab*, which is Hebrew for "returning from afar." We will see this star again in a sign which will depict Jesus coming for His people. The second brightest star is named in Hebrew *Scheat*, which is the same star we have seen in Aquarius, and means "he who goes and returns." This shows us that Aquarius and Pegasus represent the same person. In the old zodiac found at Denderah, Pegasus is represented as a human figure wearing a crown and leading the uppermost part of a horse.

There are two written characters under the horse, *Pe* and *Ka*, which is Hebrew for "chief." The third brightest star has an Arabic name, *Al Genib*, and means "who carries." Other stars are named *Enif*, which means "the branch"; *Homan*, which means "the water"; and Matar, "to cause to overflow." The star that means "the branch" testifies that Pegasus represents the same person as the branch of Virgo. The message is clear: the one who is called the branch and the chief who wears a crown is one who goes and will return quickly, joyfully. He carries water (blessings) with him which he will "cause to overflow" toward the fish (His people). This sign adds to and helps us understand Aquarius pouring out water to the fish and that he who has left us will return from afar. Jesus said he would have to leave, but He would return:

> *In my Father's house are many mansions: if it were not so, I would have told you. I go to prepare a place for you, and if I go and prepare a place for you, I will come again, and receive you unto myself, that where I am, there ye may be also* (John 14:2-3 KJV).

Pegasus confirms that the final promise of Scripture is true.

> *He which testifieth these things saith, Surely I come quickly. Amen, Even so, come Lord Jesus* (Revelation 22:20 KJV).

The next and last decan should add to this same theme and verify the sixth major sign of the zodiac, Aquarius.

Cygnus (The Swan Circling)

The last decan of Aquarius is *Cygnus*, and is pictured as a swan flying. This constellation is also known as the Northern Cross, and forms a cross bigger than the

Southern Cross. The swan in all ages has been known for its elegance, beauty, and grace. The Latin *Cygnus* means "who comes and goes," and is similar to the Greek name *Cygnos* meaning "the swan circling." So far, this sign gives us the same message as Pegasus.

Star Names of Cygnus

The brightest star in Cygnus is named in Hebrew *Deneb*, and means "the Lord or Judge cometh." Deneb was also the name of a star in Capricornus and shows us that this sign represents the same person as Capricornus does. The second brightest star is named in Arabic *Al Bireo*, meaning "flying quickly," and the third brightest is named in Hebrew *Sadr*, "who returns as in a circle." There are three more stars named in Hebrew—*Azel*, "who goes and returns quickly"; *Fafage*, meaning "the glorious shining forth"; and *Arided*, "he shall come down."

The star names declare the same message we have seen earlier. The Lord and judge is returning quickly as in a circle. When He returns, He will come down out of heaven and there will be a glorious shining forth. This is seen in Matthew 24:

> *For as the lightning cometh out of the east, and shineth even unto the west; so shall also the coming of the Son of man be* (Matthew 24:27 KJV).

> *An then shall appear the sign of the Son of man in heaven: and then all the tribes of the earth shall mourn, and they shall see the Son of man coming in the clouds of heaven with power and great glory* (Matthew 24:30 KJV).

Pisces (The Fish)

The Band (or bridle) Andromeda (The Chained Woman)

Cepeus (The King)

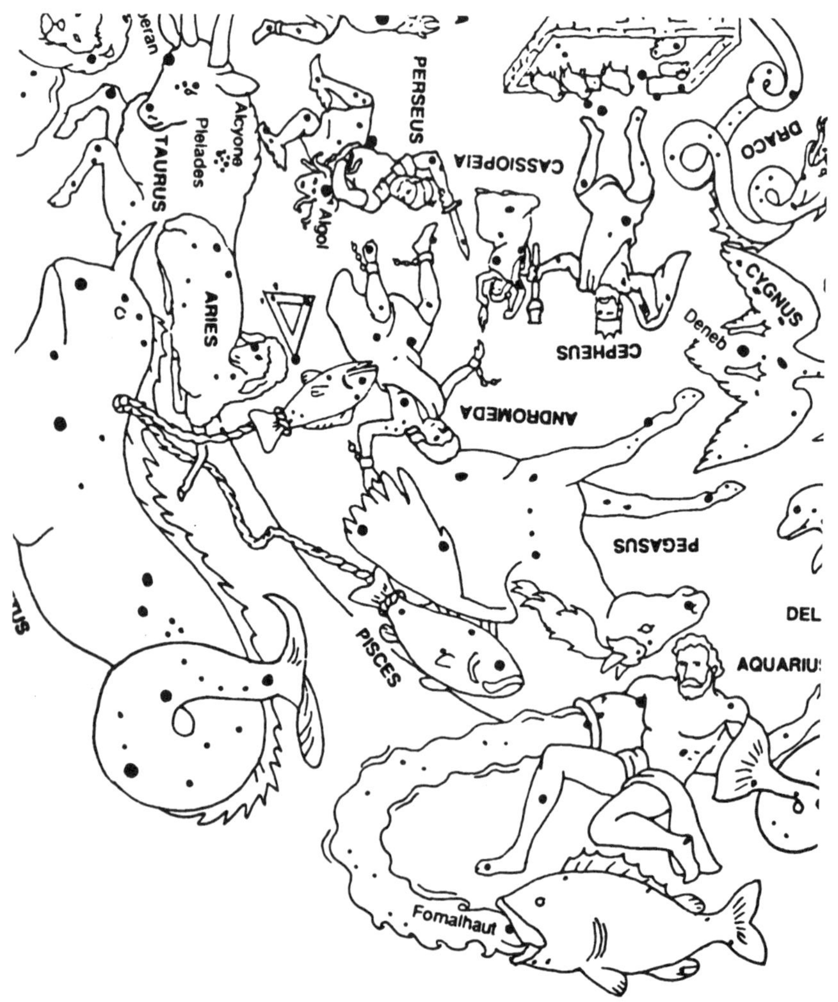

Chapter Ten

Pisces (The Fish)

The seventh major zodiacal sign is *Pisces*, and is shown as two fish tied together by another sign named the Band. This band is tied around the tail of the fishes while the middle is attached to *Cetus*, the sea monster. One fish is traveling along the path of the sun and the other is swimming up toward the pole star. We also see *Aries*, the ram (or lamb), with his foreleg placed on the band also. We have already seen that the fish symbolized the people of God in *Delphinus* and in *Piscis Australis,* "the southern fish."

If you add the two fish's size together, you will see that they are about the same size as the southern fish. Many think Pisces represents two parts of the one larger southern fish. The smaller of the two fish is swimming toward the north star and is touching Andromeda, which represents the people of God being persecuted. This tells me that the persecutions of Andromeda will happen to some of the people (fish). The larger fish is swimming toward the urn and water of Aquarius, with barely enough cord (of the band) to reach the water. The band itself is attached to the sea monster and symbolizes that this sea monster is trying to hold back the fish while the fish are holding him back also. There is a struggle, but Aries the ram (or lamb) is involved in it, too. In fact, it could be said that Aries has both the fish and the monster in his control. This will all become clearer when we look at the decans of this sign. The ancient name for this sign in Hebrew is *Dagim*, "the fish" (like a multitude) and shows that it represents a multitude of people. The name of Pisces in Denderah is *Piscis Hori*, "the fish of him who comes."

Star Names of Pisces

There are two stars named from ancient times. The first is named in Hebrew *Okda* and means "the united." The second is named in Arabic *Al Samaca*, "the upheld." This shows that the body of Christ, or the Christians, are united in Him and are upheld by Him (symbolized by Aries' foot on the band).

The Band (or Bridle)

The first decan of Pisces is *The Band,* which is separate from the sign itself and always has been seen this way. This band connects the two fish, but is also connected to the back of the sea monster with Aries touching it too. The ancient name for this sign in Arabic is *Al Risha,* "the band or bridle." The idea of a bridle helps to clear up the interaction of the signs. Aries has the bridle (reins) in his control and allows the enemy to fight with us at this time, but it is always in his control.

The enemy will bring problems, persecutions and temptations, but we have the following promise:

> *No temptation has seized you except what is common to man. And God is faithful; he will not let you be tempted beyond what you can bear. But when you are tempted, he will also provide a way out so that you can stand up under it* (I Corinthians 10:13).

Satan, who is symbolized by the sea monster, is known in Scripture as the "tempter." Satan is allowed to tempt now, but soon he will be destroyed. It should be noted that trials and temptations are tools that help us to grow:

> *Consider it pure joy, my brothers, whenever you face trials of many kinds, because you know that the testing of your faith develops perseverance. Perseverance must finish its work so that you may be mature and complete, not lacking anything* (James 1:2-4).

Star Names of the Band

The name of the only surviving star is located in the neck of Cetus and is the same name as the sign *Al Risha* (Arabic), meaning "the band or bridle." Aries (Jesus) will one day break the chains that hold back the blessings and the tempter will be no more!

Andromeda (The Chained Woman)

The second decan of Pisces is *Andromeda*, and is shown as a beautiful woman chained hand and foot. She has been abused in her captivity and her dress is torn. The ancient name for this sign in Hebrew is *Sirra* meaning "the chained." In Greek mythology, Cepheus consults the oracle for advice about what to do about Cetus, the sea monster, who was ravaging the kingdom. The oracle said that Andromeda should be chained to a rock to be devoured by Cetus. However, she was rescued by Perseus who destroyed the sea monster with the head of Medusa, and then he married Andromeda. The gospel story is found in the mythology and not too far from the absolute truth. The enemy would love to devour the Christians just like Cetus would like to devour Andromeda:

> *Be sober, be vigilant: because your adversary the devil, as a roaring lion, walketh about, seeking whom he may devour* (1 Peter 5:8 KJV).

Persus, who represents Jesus, has rescued us from our enemy, will soon totally unchain us, and we will go to the Marriage Supper of the Lamb:

> *And he saith unto me, Write, Blessed are they which are called unto the marriage supper of the Lamb* (Revelation 19:9 KJV).

In the Bible, Christians are called the Bride of

Christ. So we can see the myth still contains the elements of the original, biblical truth.

Star Names of Andromeda

The name of the brightest star in this sign is *Al Phiratz,* Arabic for "the broken down." The second brightest star bears a Hebrew name, *Mirach*, "the weak." *Al Maac*, the third brightest, means "the struck down" in Arabic. Other names are *Adhil*, "the afflicted," and *Mizar*, "the bound." The last star is named *Al Mosealah,* "delivered from the grave or hell."

These star names all mirror what we have already said, and it is absolutely amazing to see these biblical parallels. The last few scriptures we will look at will show that at least some of the body of Christ will suffer and further the truth of this sign:

> *Be self-controlled and alert. Your enemy the devil prowls around like a roaring lion looking for someone to devour. Resist him, standing firm in the faith, because you know that your brothers throughout the world are undergoing the same kind of sufferings. And the God of all grace, who called you to his eternal glory in Christ, after you have suffered a little while, will himself restore you and make you strong, firm and steadfast* (1 Peter 5:8-10)

Cepheus (The King)

The last decan of Pisces is *Cepheus* and is shown as

a bearded king sitting on a throne wearing a royal crown. He holds a scepter in one hand and a part of his robe in the other. Notice that his foot is placed upon the pole star and the "little sheep fold" is under his feet. He sits next to his wife, Cassiopea, and has his scepter stretched out to her. The pole star that Cepheus, the king's foot is on, is considered the highest point in all the heavens and the place in which all the heavens revolve around. Who is the King? Lets go to the ancient names and look for the answer. The ancient name for this sign in Hebrew is *Cepheus*, "the branch." We have found out that Jesus was called "the branch" four times in the Bible, and we first saw the star name branch *(Tsemech)* in Virgo the virgin. Remember, God has named the stars to give us a message, and He gave some stars the same name when He wanted to show that one figure actually represented another figure or figures. The Ethiopians called him *Hyk*, "the king," and at Denderah, he was called *Perku Hor*, which means "this one cometh to rule."

Star Names of Cepheus

The brightest star in Cepheus was named in Arabic *Al Deramin*, meaning "coming quickly as in a circle." This reminds us of what we have seen in Pegasus and in Cygnus (the swan circling). Other stars in Arabic are *Al Phirk,* "the redeemer," and *Al Rai,* meaning "he who bruises or breaks."

Two stars that are named in Hebrew are *Cheicus*, meaning "to come in a circle" and *Regulus*, "treading underfoot." Let's look at what the heavens have declared in this sign. There is a king who is called the branch and the redeemer who will come (return) quickly as in a circle. He is high above all the heavens and the heavens revolve around him. He comes to rule, bruise, break, and tread His enemies underfoot.

Who in all history comes close to this description while also fulfilling being born of a virgin and dying on a cross? This same person would also have to fulfill over 100 specific predictions made by people (prophets) who knew the future happenings about the Messiah because God revealed it to them. These prophets would predict where He would be born, what He would be called, and many particular things that would happen to Him, many of which would be out of His control to fulfill, humanly speaking.

The person of history who has fulfilled the biblical predictions also is described in the ancient names of the signs and stars. Jesus Christ is truly the Redeemer of mankind! God has given many signs, which present strong evidence to convince any searching person that Jesus is "the way." Remember, the word Zodiac comes from *Zodi*, which means "the way." No other religious writings in the world contain specific predictions like the Bible does! God's method has been to tell us in advance so when it came to pass we would know that He is God, and also so we would not be deceived by the enemy. Jesus is the Savior described in the Bible *and* the heavens!

Aries (The Lamb or Ram)

Cassiopeia (Woman Enthroned) Cetus (Sea Monster)
Perseus (The Breaker)

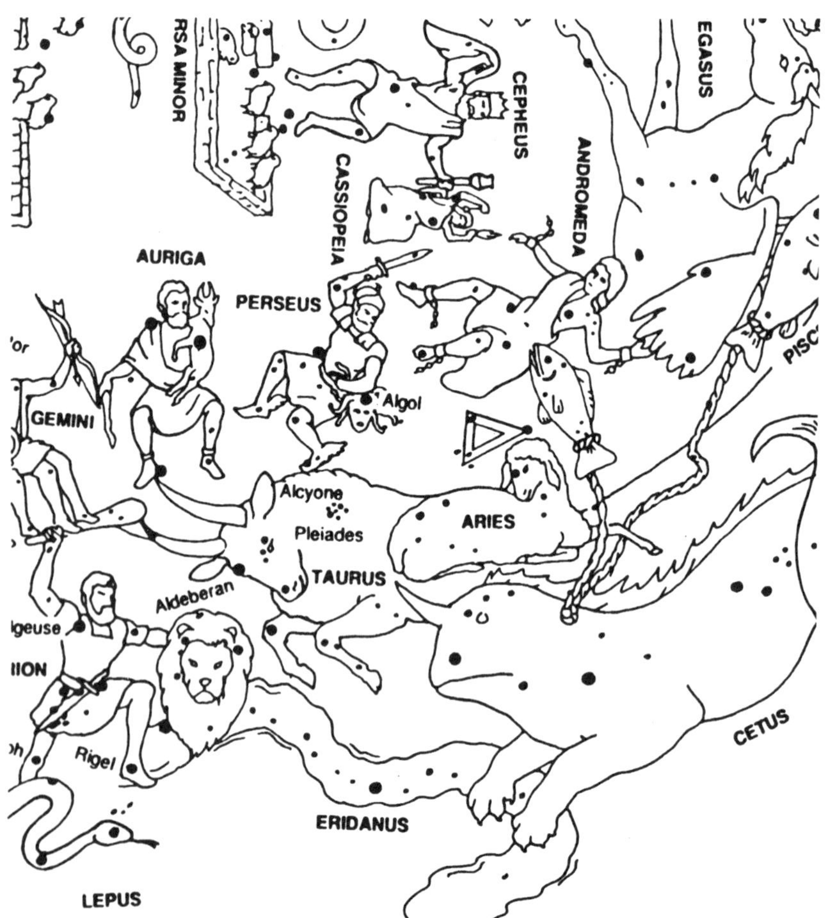

Chapter Eleven

Aries (The Lamb or Ram)

The eighth major sign of the Zodiac to declare the glory of God is named *Aries*. This is the last sign of the Second Act, which consisted of Capricorn, Aquarius, Pisces, and Aries. Capricorn showed us that life would come from death. Aquarius displayed the blessing of this new life. Pisces pictured a time of struggle, temptation, and persecution. Now Aries depicts the blessing fully realized that will happen at some time in the future.

Aries is shown as a lamb or ram resting with his head turned, looking away from the new life and water section to the next act which speaks of the second coming, judgment and glory. Aries has his left leg on the bands which are connected to Cetus and the two ends are tied to Pisces.

Astrologers begin with Aries because the sun was in Aries at the spring equinox during ancient times. The truth is that the sun has long since passed out of Aries during the spring equinox—one of many facts that invalidates astrology. Even though it is true that the enemy has conspired to cover up the truth, there is one thing the astrologer is right about: You *can* get knowledge and information from the stars. There is even knowledge that pertains to the future but not the way the astrologers understand it.

The ancient Hebrew name for this sign is *Taleh*, meaning "the lamb sent forth." The Syriac name was similar in meaning—*Amroo*, "the lamb." The Arabians confirm this sign has a lamb and not a ram by naming it *Al Hamal,* "the sheep, gentle, merciful." Remember, Jesus is called "the Lamb of God who takes away the sin of the world."

The name *Aries* has the meaning of "chief" or "head," and is pictured on some of the oldest zodiacs as a lamb with a circular crown on his head. Some of the early pictures placed a triangle above the head of Aries, and the Arabs called this triangle *Ras Al Thalita*, "the head of the triangle." Perhaps this triangle degenerated to horns on the lamb, which made it look like a ram. I am only speculating as to the reason why this lamb would be changed to the ram, but in this case, the ancient names have preserved the truth of the "crowned lamb." In the Old Testament, rams were used as sacrificial offerings, and it was a ram that Abraham sacrificed instead of his son, Isaac. Whether it is a lamb or a ram, the message is still the same.

Star Names of Aries

The brightest star in this constellation is named in Arabic *El Natik*, "the wounded or slain." The second brightest is named *Al Sheratan*, meaning "the bruised." In 1984, two astronomers figured that at the time of

Jesus' death, the sun stood near these two stars. When the supernatural darkness fell on the earth, the people of that day would have looked for the sun, but instead saw Aries, the lamb, and these two stars.

Cassiopeia (The Woman Enthroned)

The first decan of Aries is *Cassiopeia*, who is pictured as a woman seated upon her throne with her hands raised. Her right hand holds her gown and in her left hand she holds a branch. In some zodiacs she is seen brushing her hair and making herself ready for presentation. This woman represents the church (the Bride of Christ) who has been lifted out of the bondage represented in Andromeda and placed upon a throne next to her king and husband. King Cepheus holds out his scepter of approval to her. The ancient name for this sign in Hebrew is "the enthroned, the beautiful." The Chaldean and Arabic names are the same, *Dat Al Cursa,* meaning "set up" (as queen).

Star Names of Cassiopeia

The brightest star in this sign is named in Hebrew *Shedar*, "the freed" and is in contrast to Andromeda, whose name means "the chained" in Hebrew. Another star with a Hebrew name, located in the back of the throne, is *Caph*, meaning "the branch." The throne belongs to the branch and this queen has been set upon it. From an astronomical point of view, this sign looks like a "w" and it never sets on the horizon (indicating this throne is forever).

Cetus (The Sea Monster)

The second decan of Aries is *Cetus*, and is represented as a fierce looking sea monster—another pictorial representative of our enemy Satan. This is the largest constellation in the sky and in mythology it was Cetus who was sent to devour Andromeda. Satan (Cetus) would love to devour the Church (as represented by Andromeda), but Perseus has rescued her as we shall see in the next sign. The Egyptians called Cetus *Knem*, which means "subdued." The band of Pisces is attached to his back and the lamb (Aries) has his leg on this band (bridle). The lamb keeps him from doing all that he would like to do to the fish (Pisces). What does this monster do to the fish or fish people? Satan is known as the tempter in the Bible and it is he who brings trials and persecutions to God's people. He would love to devour us but he cannot. The lamb only allows him to do so much and the Christian has been strengthened against the enemy:

> *There hath no temptation taken you but such as is common to man: but God is faithful, who will not suffer you to be tempted above that ye are able; but will with the temptation also make a way to escape, that ye may be able to bear it* (1 Corinthians 10:13 KJV).

Peter gave us instructions about what to do against this enemy:

> *Be sober, he vigilant; because your adversary the devil, as a roaring lion, walketh about, seeking whom he may devour* (I Peter 5:8 KJV).

Saint Paul also instructed us about what to do to protect ourselves from him:

> *Finally, my brethren, be strong in the Lord, and in the power of his might. Put on the whole armor of God, that ye may be able to stand against the wiles of the devil, For we wrestle not against flesh and blood, but against principalities, against powers, against the rulers of the darkness of this world, against spiritual wickedness in high places* (Ephesians 6:10-12 KJV).

Star Names of Cetus

The brightest star in Cetus is *Menkar*, which is Hebrew for "the bound or chained." Another Hebrew named star is *Diphda*, meaning "the overthrown." These star names accurately describe Satan and his end in Isaiah 26 and Revelation 20:

> *For, behold, the LORD cometh out of his place to punish the inhabitants of the earth for their iniquity: the earth also shall disclose her blood, and shall no more cover her slain* (Isaiah 26:21 KJV).

In that day the LORD with his sore and great and strong sword shall punish leviathan the piercing serpent, even leviathan that crooked serpent; and he shall slay the dragon that is in the sea (Isaiah 27:1 KJV).

And in Revelation 20:1-3:

And I saw an angel come down from heaven, having the key of the bottomless pit and a great chain in his hand. And he laid hold on the dragon, that old serpent, which is the Devil, and Satan, and bound him a thousand years, And cast him into the bottomless pit, and shut him up, and set a seal upon him that he should deceive the nations no more, till the thousand years should be fulfilled: and after that he must he loosed a little season (KJV).

The most interesting star in Cetus is named *Mira*, which is Hebrew for “the rebel.” Satan is the first rebel in the universe and the leader of the rebellion against God. This star was discovered to be a variable star in the years 1596-1648 by various astronomers. It becomes visible and then invisible on a regular period of about 11 months. It is invisible to the naked eye most of the time. There may be a special lesson taught in this for us to understand. Rebellion is only a temporary thing. God will ultimately stamp it out, even as this star is visible only temporarily. Also the enemy likes to remain invisible and undetected most of the time. Usually he is only revealed when God exposes him. Satan is revealed in the Zodiac as Scorpio the scorpion, Serpens the serpent, Draco the dragon, the triple-headed Hydra in Hercules, and now Cetus, the sea monster. Before the revelation of the stars is complete, he will be spoken of a few more times. In Denderah, the figure is named *Knem*, "the subdued" or "the bruised."

Perseus (The Breaker)

The third decan of Aries and last figure in this second act of the heavens is *Perseus*, which is shown as a mighty helmeted man coming on the run with a sword in his left hand and the head of an enemy in his right hand. On his ankles are wings, showing that he comes with supernatural speed. His name in Greek is Perseus, which comes from a Hebrew word, *Peretz*, meaning "the breaker." In the old Denderah zodiac, his name is *Kar Knem*, meaning "the one who fights the subdued or bruised." We saw Knem in Cetus and discovered that it was another name for Cetus and meant, "the subdued or bruised."

Star Names of Perseus

The brightest star in Perseus is *Mirfak* (Hebrew), meaning "he who helps." A star located in his left foot has a Hebrew name, *Athik*, "he who breaks." Another star in Arabic is *Al Genib,* "he who carries away." The Greeks said that Perseus chopped off Medusa's head and is carrying it. They did not know the Hebrew word meant, "the trodden underfoot." The star in the head of

Medusa, in Hebrew, was called *Rosh Satan,* "the head of the adversary, or the head of Satan." Amazing! Remember, this heavenly story was recorded before the Bible was written.

Arabians had two names for the head: *Al Oneh,* meaning "the subdued" (Cetus was called the subdued) and *Al Ghoul*, "the evil spirit." The Arabians called the bright star in the head by a contraction of the name we just saw, *Algol*, meaning "coming and going, rolling around the head." This star also acts like a variable star by changing magnitudes from a maximum of mag. 2.3 to a minimum of mag. 3.3. This star changes like Mira in Cetus, but unlike Mira, it always remains visible to the naked eye. The period of change is about every two days and 21 hours. This star will begin to drop, and in four hours will be at a minimum for 20 minutes, and then goes back up to maximum. In a little more than eight hours, it will "wink" at you. Perhaps that is why the Arabians named it "coming and going." This star in the head of Satan speaks of how the devil changes his appearance even "transforming himself into an angel of light." In contrast, Jesus Christ "is the same yesterday, today, and forever." We have seen our soon coming king dressed as a warrior having subdued the enemy and rescuing us. Now we go to the final act in the heavenly revelation.

Taurus (The Bull or Wild Ox)

Orion (The Hunter) Eridanus (The River)
Auriga (The Shepherd)

Chapter Twelve

Taurus (The Bull or Wild Ox)

The ninth major sign of the zodiac is named *Taurus*, who is shown as the front half of a mighty charging bull that has long, sharp horns. This bull has his head lowered, as if he is about to gore something. The upper horn of Taurus is piercing the heel of *Auriga*, the shepherd, and the lower horn is touching the club of *Orion*, the hunter. What kind of bull is this? Taurus represents a now extinct, fierce relative of domestic cattle and was called a *Rimu* in Hebrew. Rimu is translated "unicorn" in the Bible, and was thought to be a one-horned animal. It is now known to be an animal much larger and fiercer than the cattle of today and most modern versions of the Bible call it a wild ox. It was hunted by Egyptian kings and survived until the time of the Caesars. Caesar wrote of the hunters of his day proving their ability by killing one and then exhibiting the horn of the rimu. The book of Job was written around 1500 B.C. and describes a rimu.

Will the unicorn [rimu] *be willing to serve thee,*

> *or abide by thy crib? Canst thou bind the unicorn with his band in the furrow? or will he harrow the valleys after thee?* (Job 39:9-10 KJV).

There are many scriptures in the Bible that prove that this bull or wild ox is extremely strong, untamable, and history shows it almost the size of an elephant. The name for this sign in Hebrew is *Shur*, "the bull coming," and *Rimu,* which, as we saw, is the same word used in the Bible that is interpreted unicorn or wild ox. This wild ox was also spoken of in connection with judgment:

> *For the indignation of the Lord is upon all nations, and His fury upon all their armies: he hath utterly destroyed them, he hath delivered them to the slaughter* (Isaiah 34:2 KJV).

> *For my sword shall be bathed in heaven: behold, it shall come down upon Idumea, and upon the people of my curse, to judgment* (Isaiah 34:5 KJV).

> *And the unicorns shall come down with them, and the bullocks with the bulls; and their land shall be soaked with blood, and their dust made fat with fatness* (Isaiah 34:7 KJV).

Keeping all this in mind, what is the message of Taurus? Taurus speaks of the mighty judgment of God coming, and the wrath of God that will be poured out on

His enemies. We know that the day of the Lord is coming and all those who have not received the Son of God, but have rejected Him, have only the wrath of God to look forward to. But the Christian has no need to fear because of the many promises in the Word of God, one of which is below:

> *And to wait for his Son from heaven, whom he raised from the dead—Jesus, who rescues us from the coming wrath* (1 Thessalonians 1:10).

The decan signs of Taurus will illustrate this message even more.

Star Names of Taurus

The brightest star in Taurus is *Al Debaran* and means "the leader" or "governor." The second brightest is *El Nath,* which is Arabic for "the wounded" or "the slain." This star is located in the upper horn of Taurus, which is pricking the heel of *Auriga*, "the Shepherd." This same star, *El Nath*, was also the name of a star in Aries which shows that Aries and Taurus represent the same person. Another star was named *Al Cylone,* which is in the Pleiades and means "the center." The Pleiades are a cluster of seven stars that the Hebrews called *Chima*, "the accumulation." These stars were associated with the flood of Noah and the judgment poured out by God. Taurus was also recognized with the flood of Noah (where only the righteous were saved), and the evidence is found in the astronomical symbol for Taurus—♉ .

Those who are hieroglyphic authorities describe it as a single boat on the surface of the earth. The *Hyades* a cluster of stars that is located in the left red eye of the bull means "the congregated" in Hebrew. (In the Bible, the true believer is called "the apple of His eye.") Another star which has a Hebrew name is *Palilicum*, "belonging to the judge."

The last star we will look at is *Wasat* in Arabic, or "the foundation." This star gives us a clue as to the true meaning along with the fact that the Pleiades is located in the shoulder of the bull.

Let's look at what the Bible says about Jesus:

> *For unto us a child is born, unto us a son is given: and the government shall be upon his shoulder: and his name shall be called Wonderful, Counsellor, the Mighty God, the Everlasting Father, the Prince of Peace* (Isaiah 9:6 KJV).

The first decan sign of Taurus is *Orion* and is pictured as a mighty man. Let's look at one more scripture and then we can make sense of it all:

> *Now therefore ye are no more strangers and foreigners, but fellow citizens with the saints, and of the household of God; And are built upon the foundation of the apostles and prophets, Jesus Christ himself being the chief corner stone; In whom all the building fitly framed together groweth unto an holy temple in the Lord: In*

whom ye also are builded together for an habitation of God through the Spirit (Ephesians 2:19-22 KJV).

In the government of Jesus, we shall rule with Him as kings and priests. The Syriac name for the Pleiades is *Succoth*, which means "booths," and reminds us of the Israeli feast of booths or tabernacles. The Pleiades are known as the seven sisters and the feast of booths is to be celebrated seven days. This feast represents prophetically a time when God will tabernacle with men. The full significance of this is yet to be discovered.

Orion (The Hunter)

The first decan sign of Taurus is *Orion* and is pictured as a mighty man who has a club uplifted about to strike his enemy. This club is in his right hand and is aimed in the general direction of Cetus. The lower horn of Taurus is touching the club and shows they both have the same function—judgment. In Orion's left hand, he holds the severed head of a lion, which he has killed. He wears a belt and sword (which are well known), and his left foot is uplifted ready to crush the head of his enemy, The river *Eridanus* also begins at this same foot. On the hilt of his sword is the figure of a lamb, which helps to identify him with the lamb of Aries. Orion, in mythology, was known as a mighty hunter who had supernatural powers. He could walk on water and was known as a hero. Apollo sent Scorpius, the scorpion to attack Orion, and in some accounts, the scorpion killed

Orion by stinging his foot. In this story, the Bible revelation still shines through the corrupt myth. Orion is the Hebrew name for this sign with the meaning "one coming forth as light." The Arabs called him *Al Mazam*, "the prince, the ruler," and also *Al Nagjed*, "the prince, the wounded." The Accadian name is similar to the Hebrew name—*Urana,* "the light of heaven."

Star Names of Orion

The brightest star in Orion is the splendid orange-red *Betelguez*, located in his right shoulder, and means "the coming of the branch." We have noted earlier the first mention of the branch is in Virgo, and that God would include this same name as well as others in different signs to show that we are talking about the same person (who was born of a virgin).

The second brightest star is the brilliantly white *Rigel* (*Rigol*), which means "the foot that crushes." This star is located in the left foot of Orion, which is uplifted ready to crush. Another star is *Bellatrix*, which means "quickly coming." The star in his right leg has a Hebrew name, *Saiph*, which means "bruised." We saw this star in Orphiucus, and in fact, Orion reminds us of Orphiucus and also Hercules. Look at the star map and you will see what I mean. There are many more names which all point to the branch, the prince, the light of heaven, the ruler, and the wounded.

Eridanus (The River)

The second decan sign of Taurus is *Eridanus*, which

is a river that flows in a crooked path from the raised foot of Orion to the paws of Cetus and then out of sight. What is the message in the river in connection with the other signs we have seen? This river has its beginning at the raised foot of Orion, which tells us that they both have a similar purpose. The foot of Orion has the same purpose as the foot of Orphiucus and Hercules, to bring the predicted judgment on the enemy (to crush his head, or, in other words, to defeat him). Taurus and Orion speak of judgment and now this sign does too. *Eridanus* is a Hebrew name and means "river of the judge." The Greeks saw this as a river of fire and some other authors of this subject depict it as a river of life. The following scripture clears all this up for us:

> *Who can withstand his indignation? Who can endure his fierce anger? His wrath is poured out like fire; the rocks are shattered before him* (Nahum 1:6).

This constellation graphically speaks of the final judgment in which the wicked will be cast into the lake of fire along with Satan (who is represented by Cetus).

Star Names of Eridanus

The brightest star in this sign, *Achernar*, means "the afterpart of the river," and is located in the half of the river past Cetus. This shows that it flows from Orion toward Cetus and then to the horizon of "outermost darkness." The second brightest is *Cursa*, Hebrew for "bent down," and the last is *Zourak*, which is Arabic for "flowing." The idea of judgment gives way to hope in the next sign.

Auriga (The Shepherd)

The third decan sign of Taurus is *Auriga* who is a gentle shepherd that contrasts the mighty Taurus and Orion. Auriga is about the same size as Orion and the outer stars are similar in shape when you include *Elnath*, which is in the heel of the shepherd or horn of Taurus. The horns of Taurus speak of judgment and it can be seen that judgment has come to this shepherd in his heel. This sign shows that this shepherd took judgment for the sheep, lambs, or goats. Notice the shepherd is holding a mother goat and her kids safely protected from the mighty bull. This truth was given to us by the mouth of Jesus in John 10:

> *I am the good shepherd. The good shepherd lays down his life for the sheep* (John 10:11).

Yes, He laid down His life, but look what else happened:

> *No one takes it from me, but I lay it down of my own accord. I have authority to lay it down and authority to take it up again. This command I received from my Father* (John 10:18).

If Jesus died and was buried and that was it, there would be no hope for us, but he has been raised and is alive forevermore!

Prophetically speaking, this shepherd rounds out the picture of the coming of the Lord in great power, glory, judgment and mercy for His own people. In the shepherd's right hand are reins which relate to the bands of Pisces and identifies him with Aries who also holds the reins of the fish people. The goats or sheep here represent the people of God, the same as the fish do in Aries. The Hebrews called this sign *Auriga*, the Shepherd, and the same word is used in Isaiah 40:11:

> *Behold, the LORD God will come with strong hand, and his arm shall rule for him: behold, his reward is with him, and his work before him, He shall feed his flock like a shepherd: he shall gather the lambs with his arm, and carry them in his bosom, and shall gently lead those that are with young* (Isaiah 40:10-11 KJV).

This scripture sums up the message of this sign. The Greeks called this sign *Haeniochos*, "the driver or charioteer," which is probably the source for it being known in modern times as "the wagoneer." This is an inaccurate name and comes from the Latin name *Auriga*, which means "the conductor of the reins." From this you can see how, through time, the true names of the stars and constellations would get distorted from the truth. This would happen by accident sometimes, but the evil one has conspired to change and distort the message of the heavens. This is the reason I once titled this book *The Zodiac Conspiracy.* The stars will confirm the meaning of this sign as a shepherd.

Star Names of Auriga

The brightest star in this sign is named *Capella*, which is Latin for the "she-goat," and the Hebrews called this same star *Alioth*, "the ewe or she-goat." Another star named in Hebrew was *Gedi*, meaning "the kids." The second brightest star is in his right arm, *Menkalinon*, which is Chaldean for "the band of the goats or ewes." Don't forget the star *El Nath*, which, although it is in Taurus, many believe it was originally in Auriga, and it means "the wounded." Everywhere you look, the Gospel story is seen and confirmed in the heavens. Many people think astrology, psychics, and almost anything supernatural is of God, and yet nothing could be further from the truth. The Bible teaches that we must be discerning between what is of God and what is of the enemy. We have been given the warning that Satan can transform himself into an "angel of light" to deceive. The more of the Bible you know, the more discernment you will have. We have also been warned that false prophets and false teachers will deceive many and we see this happening now. It is the Bible that gives us the insight to understand what "the heavens declare" and what "the line and words" of the heavens reveal:

> *Their line is gone out through all the earth, and their words to the end of the world* (Psalms 19:4).

Gemini (The Twins)

Lepus (Snake) Canis Major (Greater Dog or Prince)
Canis Minor (Lesser Dog or Coming Redeemer)

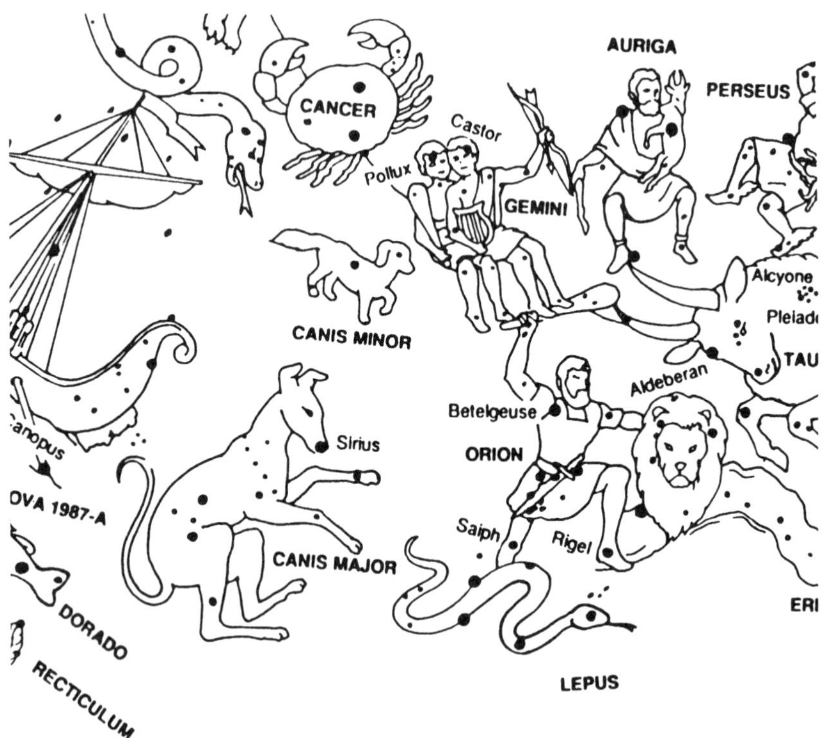

Chapter Thirteen

Gemini (The Twins)

The tenth major sign of the zodiac is *Gemini*—the two famous twin youths sitting side by side. The twin on the left is holding a club and the one on the right holds an unstrung bow in his left hand and a harp in his right. The figure on the left is named *Pollux* or *Hercules*, and the figure on the right is named *Castor* or *Apollo*. In mythology, these two were great heroes who sailed with the Argonauts in the quest for the golden fleece. They also removed pirates from the seas and made them safe to sail and are, therefore, honored among seamen. They were also honored as kings and saviors. The Denderah zodiac is pictured as a man leading a woman by the hand.

The ancient names will help us see the meaning of this sign. The Hebrews named this sign *Thaumin*, "the united." This name, along with the Arabic and Syriac names, carry the idea of completion, like the completion of a betrothal. The Hebrew name above is used in Exodus 26:24, and refers to boards which are to be "twinned" and made to be alike.

Star Names of Gemini

The brightest star in this sign is *Castor*, a Greek and also Latin word meaning "the ruler" or "judge." The second brightest is *Pollux*, meaning "who comes to labor and suffer." Pollux is carrying a club in the relaxed position and in some old zodiacs, he carries a branch. In the foot of Pollux is *Al Henah* meaning the "hurt." Another Hebrew named star is *Mebsuta*, "treading underfoot." This reminds me of one of my favorite scriptures in the Bible found in Romans:

> *The God of peace will soon crush Satan under your feet. The grace of our Lord Jesus be with you* (Romans 16:20).

Because the feet of Gemini are touching the club of Orion, it seems that the feet serve the same purpose as the club, and the above scripture gives us the true understanding of this symbolism. Another star in Arabic is *Wasat*, meaning "established as a foundation" or *Set*, or "appointed to rule."

Two Arabic names for the stars are *Al Giauza*, "the palm branch," and *Al Dira,* "the seed." There is a star, named in Hebrew, *Propus*, "the branch spreading." This sign speaks of a uniting of the church to her Savior. We are to be in the image of Christ and join the battle bearing arms, singing praises on the harp, and will one day rule together with Him. Jesus is the seed and the branch which we first saw in Virgo, the virgin. This sign also speaks of Jesus in His dual role as ruler and sufferer.

We also share in all these things. We will rule with him in Revelation 20:4:

> *And I saw thrones, and they sat upon them, and judgment was given unto them: and I saw the souls of them that were beheaded for the witness of Jesus, and for the word of God, and which had not worshipped the beast, neither his image, neither had received his mark upon their foreheads, or in their hands, and they lived and reigned with Christ a thousand years.*

We must also share in His sufferings sometimes:

> *And if children, then heirs; heirs of God, and joint-heirs with Christ; if so be that we suffer with him, that we may be also glorified together* (Romans 8:17 KJV).

> *For unto you it is given in the behalf of Christ not only to believe on him, but also to suffer for his sake* (Philippians 1:29 KJV).

Lepus (The Snake)

The first decan of Gemini is *Lepus*, and is pictured as a snake on the run. Most star charts have pictured this as a hare on the run, but a few have the snake. Orion, the mighty Orphicius, and Hercules are crushing the head of the enemy. The star above the head of Lepus and in the raised foot of Orion means "the foot that crushes." This takes us back to Genesis 3:14-15:

> *And the LORD God said unto the serpent. Because thou hast done this, thou art cursed above all cattle, and above every beast of the field; upon thy belly shalt thy go and dust shalt thou eat all the days of thy life: And I will put enmity between thee and the woman, and between thy seed and her seed; he shall bruise thy head, and thou shalt bruise his heel* (KJV).

In Orion's other leg is a star named *Saiph,* which means "bruised." It is obvious that the stars speak of Jesus and Genesis 3:15. The Hebrews called this sign *Arnebo*, "the enemy of him that cometh." The Arabs called him *Arnbeth*, meaning "the hare, the enemy of him that cometh." Perhaps here is where the confusion of a hare first started. The star names will show that this is the enemy and in my opinion should be represented with a snake and not a hare (rabbit).

Star Names of Lepus

The brightest star in this sign is *Arnebo*, and we have seen it means "the enemy of him that cometh." There are three star names that confirm this as the enemy: *Sugia*, "the deceiver"; *Nihal*, "the mad"; and *Rakis,* "the bound" (as with a chain). Satan is the deceiver and he certainly is mad and will be "bound":

> *And I saw an angel coming down out of heaven, having the key to the Abyss and holding in his hand a great chain. He seized the dragon, that*

ancient serpent, who is the devil, or Satan, and bound him for a thousand years (Revelation 20:1).

Canis Major (The Greater Dog or The Prince)

The second decan sign of Gemini is *Canis Major,* who is pictured as a dog sitting with his paws extended toward the snake. Its bright star *Sirius* is known as the "dog star" in modern times, and because of this, I decided not to depict this sign as it should be shown: "a prince on the throne." In Greek mythology, they showed Orion with a pair of hunting dogs, and this was supposedly one of his faithful dogs. The Hebrews called this sign by the same name as its brightest star, Sirius, which means "the prince." The Egyptians called this sign *Sew*, "the prince" and both of these are used in Isaiah 9:6:

For unto us a child is born, unto us a son is given: and the government shall be upon his shoulder: and his name shall be called Wonderful, Counsellor, the Mighty God, the Everlasting Father, the Prince of Peace (Isaiah 9:6 KJV).

The Names of the Stars

The brightest star in this sign is Sirius, and we have seen it means "the prince." The second brightest star had an Arabic name, *Mirzam*, "the prince." Other Arabic names are *Wezea* or *Wesen*, "the bright or shining, *Al Shira Al Jemeniya*, "the prince of the right hand." We have looked at the right hand figure of Gemini and saw it was named Pollux, which means "to come to labor and suffer." Other star names are *Al Habor,* "the might"; *Muliphen*, "the leader or chief"; and *Aschere*, "who shall come." This sign speaks of a coming prince of the right hand who is bright, shining, and the leader, ruler, and judge. Jesus sits at the right hand of God in heaven and this sign represents Him.

Canis Minor (The Lesser Dog or Coming Redeemer)

The third decan of Gemini is *Canis Minor,* and is shown as a smaller dog, but was known in ancient times as *Procyon*, "the redeemer, savior." Again, in this case the true meaning shows up in the names and not in the pictures. The ancient names have gone through less changes than some of the signs have through the years because the sign pictures were more at the mercy of every astronomer who copied them.

Star Names of Canis Minor

The brightest star in this sign is named in Hebrew *Procyon*, "the redeemer," and is also the name they called this constellation. This same star in Arabic was known as *Al Shira Al Shemeliya*, "the prince of the left hand," which is speaking of Castor, the twin on the left hand. Canis Major spoke of Pollux, the prince of the right hand. Another star name in this sign is *Al Gomesa* (Arabic) and means "burdened or bearing for others."

Jesus bore our burdens for us at Calvary when He died on the cross!

> *He was despised and rejected by men, a man of sorrows, and familiar with suffering. Like one from whom men hide their faces he was despised, and we esteemed him not. Surely he took up our infirmities and carried our sorrows, yet we considered him stricken by God, smitten by him, and afflicted. But he was pierced for our transgressions, he was crushed for our iniquities; the punishment that brought us peace was upon him, and by his wounds we are healed* (Isaiah 53:3-5).

This sign shows Jesus in His role as suffering Savior. We have seen the twins of Gemini show us the twofold nature and work of the coming Messiah, and the last two decans expand this theme. There are also overtones in the last two signs that show the Church is made like the Savior and will rule with Him. There are some who believe that the original picture of this sign should be Castor standing. In Denderah, there is a human with the head of a hawk and a tail is on him too, which means "this one comes." The hawk's head signifies that the one who comes is the natural enemy of the serpent. If this overtone interpretation is correct, then the Church is the lesser dog (prince of the left hand). There are reasons to believe that this sign speaks of both the redeemer and the redeemed! When this sign shall ultimately be fulfilled, we shall be like Him and will be one with Him!

Cancer (The Crab)

Ursa Minor (Lesser Sheepfold)

Ursa Major (Greater Sheepfold)

Argo (The Ship; The Mystery Rapture Signs)

Chapter Fourteen

Cancer (The Crab)

The eleventh major sign of the zodiac is *Cancer* and is shown as a crab facing Leo. The stars of Cancer are not easily seen at night, but this sign lies half-way between Gemini and Leo, making it easier to find than other dim constellations. This crab has many legs which in hieroglyphics indicates a multitude or multiplication. The body of Christ is a many-membered body. The pinchers of the crab are used for holding things tightly. With all this in mind, I do not believe that this was the original sign, although even the crab tells the true story. It more likely was a sheepfold and when we are finished looking at the ancient names and decan signs, there will be no doubt as to its message, even though we are not sure of the picture.

Cancer in Arabic comes from the word *Khan*, which means "the travellers resting place," and *Cer*, which means "encircled" or "embraced." The Egyptians called this sign in Coptic *Klaria*, "the cattle folds." The Greeks called it *Karkinos*, "the crab holding and encircling the possession." It's obvious that this sign speaks of a sheep fold for sheep, a cattle fold for cattle, or a resting place for a weary traveller (perhaps an inn). More clues are in the star names.

Star Names of Cancer

The brightest star in this sign is named in Hebrew and in Arabic *Acubene*, "the sheltering or hiding place. Another name for this same star is *Ma Alaph*, which means "assembled thousands."

The next brightest star is named in Hebrew *Teqmine*, "the fold or holding." Another star is named in Arabic *Al Himarein,* "the kids or lambs." The *Praesepe*, a star cluster visible to the naked eye, is called "the beehive" by modern astronomers, but the ancient Hebrew name means "the multitude, the offspring." This sign speaks of a time when the travellers are safe and secure at home. This heavenly prophetic picture displays the Bible truth of a time when we Christians will be safe and secure in our heavenly home. This sign also shows that we are embraced and a possession. The decan signs will expand this theme.

Ursa Minor (The Lesser Sheepfold)

The first decan of Cancer is *Ursa Minor* and is known as "the little bear." It has a companion, Ursa Major, "the great bear." They are also known as "the little dipper" and "the big dipper" to the people in America.

We have pictured this constellation as a sheepfold under the feet of Cephus, the king, because this is closer to the true message the ancient names give. The picture of a bear goes no further back than the Greeks. The bears in these two signs have long, raised tails which is not true of bears. The idea of a bear seems to have come from a misunderstanding of words. The old Persian word for bear is similar to the word for sheepfold, and the Greeks mistakenly took one word for the other. The Greeks called this sign *Aracs* or *Arctos*, which means "bear," but the root meaning is "the stronghold of the saved." In fact, these words in Latin mean "the travelling company." The Hebrews called this sign *Kochab*, meaning "waiting him who cometh." There are many other names for this sign, but none speak of a bear.

Star names of Ursa Minor

The brightest star in this sign is named *Cynosura*, meaning "the center." This same star is known as the pole star today, but was not in ancient times. The pole star was located in Draco over 4,000 years ago, and yet this star still was named the center! There has been a change in the spirit realm from the Dragon to Cephus, the king (Jesus). The Arabs called this same star *Al Ruccaba*, "the pole star." The amazing thing is how could the ancients know that this star would become the star that the heavens would revolve around? The answer is that they did not know it, but God did when He named the stars originally and gave this revelation to man. The second brightest is *Kochab*, which means "waiting him who cometh." Another star in Arabic is *Al Kaid,* "the assembled." All the names agree with Cancer that we are the assembled sheep of His fold, waiting Him who cometh.

Ursa Major (The Greater Sheepfold)

The second decan sign of Cancer is *Ursa Major* and is known as the greater bear, the plough in some places, and in America it is called the big dipper. Its original form was that of a sheepfold and continues the message of Cancer. The Hebrews called it *Ash*, "the assembled," and the Arabs called it *Al Naish,* "the assembled together" (as in a sheepfold),

Star Names of Ursa Major

The brightest star in this sign is named *Dubheh*, "a herd of animals." The Greeks may have mistaken the Persian word *Dob* (Hebrew *Dowb*), which means "bear," for this star which means "a herd."

Merach (Hebrew) means "the flock," and this star is named the same in Arabic with this meaning, "the purchased." This sign so far is speaking of the people of God.

Another star, *Phacda*, means "guarded, numbered." We are like the stars in heaven which are named and numbered. There is *El Acola* (Arabic), for "the sheepfold" and *Dubheh*, "the latter flock." There are many other names which all point to the same conclusion. This sign is symbolic of the sheep (people) of God who are assembled and guarded, and the purchased, who are safe and secure. The Egyptians named this sign *Fent Har,* "the one who terrifies the serpent." This speaks of the Christian who can resist the devil, and the devil will flee as in terror!

Argo (The Ship)

The third and final decan of Cancer is *Argo*, and is pictured as a ship with its sails up and oars backward, showing it is docking. This is the ship of mythology that carried Jason and the Argonauts in their quest for the golden fleece. Jason recovered the great treasure from the serpent who guarded it. The name Argo means "the company of travellers." This ship has gone on its dangerous journey with its crew, made it through all the problems and trials, and is now safe in its home port. Argo represents the travellers safely home, having won the victory. This ship has the figure of a man's face at the waterline, who seems to be carrying the ship on his back. Some have seen this as a picture of Noah's Ark, which in the time of the flood saved Noah from the wrath of God poured out on all the earth. In the same way this ship will save the true believers from the wrath of God that is to come on the earth soon (as seen in the book of Revelation).

The Names of the Stars

The brightest star in this sign is *Canopus*, "the possession of him who cometh." The star *Markab* means "returning from afar." There is prophecy in this star name because you can't return unless you leave. Jesus has come and left, and now we are looking for His return. There are stars with Hebrew names, *Sephina*, "the multitude," and *Amidiska*, "the released who travel." Two stars in Arabic are *Soheil*, "the desired, and *Subilion*, "the branch."

The names of the stars declare that this ship represents a company of travellers, actually a multitude of travellers, who are the possession of Him who cometh. This released multitude belongs to the desired one and the branch whom we first saw in Virgo, the virgin. Most people agree that this represents the catching away or rapture of the Church which is described in the following two scriptures. Take your time reading these for I will soon reveal one of the greatest modern mysteries of the signs:

> *Listen, I tell you a mystery: We will not all sleep, but we will all be changed in a flash, in the twinkling of an eye, at the last trumpet. For the trumpet will sound, the dead will be raised imperishable, and we will be changed. For the perishable must clothe itself with the imperishable, and the mortal with immortality. When the perishable has been clothed with the imperishable, and the mortal with immortality, then the saying that is written will come true: "Death has been swallowed up in victory"* (I Corinthians 15:51-54).

> And the second scripture:

> *For this we say unto you by the word of the Lord that we which are alive and remain unto the coming of the Lord shall not prevent* [precede] *them which are asleep. For the Lord Himself will descend from heaven with a shout, with the voice of the archangel and with the trump of God and the dead in Christ shall rise first: Then*

> *we which are alive and remain shall be caught up together with them in the clouds to meet the Lord in the air: and so shall we ever be with the Lord* (1 Thessalonians 4:15 KJV).

In 1987, I had been studying the stars for almost two years and understood most of what I now know, when I heard about a supernova (an exploding star) that happened in the large magellanic cloud. This star became visible to the naked eye and is the first observed supernova since 1604 to do so. I decided that there is probably a message in it for us today because I remembered the star the wise men (Magi) saw. The star they saw had also become visible to the naked eye and appeared to come out of nowhere. I spent three months researching this star and its surrounding constellations, and what I found is nothing short of astounding!

You will notice on the star chart under Argo there are two clouds, "the large and small Magellanic clouds." The new star happened in the large cloud and is scientifically called Supernova 1987A. To the right of the large cloud is *Dorado*. In the book, *The North Star to the Southern Cross,* it says Dorado represents a large species of goldfish that changes color on death. This amazed me because the fish in the Zodiac represent the people of God, and I know that at the catching away into the clouds, we will be changed! Below Dorado is *Recticulum*, which represents a net. The last sign in all of this that fits the scripture is *Volans*, "the flying fish."

Let's put it together and see what we have. The net is going to catch up the fish into the ship that is waiting in the clouds! Dorado shows that we shall be changed. This is a perfect picture of the catching away of the people of God, according to the two scriptures above! Volans is much smaller than Dorado, and I wondered if these two fish represented two different companies of people. Then it dawned on me that the Bible says that "the dead in Christ shall rise first," and this was represented by the smaller fish, Volans, because it is closer to the ship.

Then the Bible continues by saying "and then we who are alive and remain shall be caught up together with them to meet the Lord in the air." I realized that Dorado represented those of us who would be alive at the catching away. The smaller Volans shows that the dead in Christ will be a smaller company than those who are alive and remain. It is true that there are more Christians alive today than have died in Christ. So we have a ship, clouds, a goldfish that changes color at death, a net and a small flying fish—everything needed to picture this catching away and all under the correct ancient sign Argo. Coincidence? Not hardly. Remember, I only looked in this area because of the new star.

We know that the Lord is coming soon and we don't need a new message from heaven about it, and yet God even has the heavens revealing to us that the time of the catching away is soon. This is the next event to unfold on God's eternal calendar of events that He wrote in the heavens for all to see. Remember the Scripture says "Behold I tell you a mystery," and perhaps these signs were a hidden mystery to be revealed at this time. If you are not a Christian, then you should be convinced by now that you need to be. Jesus said, "You must be born again." Why not read the information at the end of this book to see how you can be saved.

Leo (The Lion)

Hydra (The Serpent) Crater (The Cup)

Corvis (The Raven)

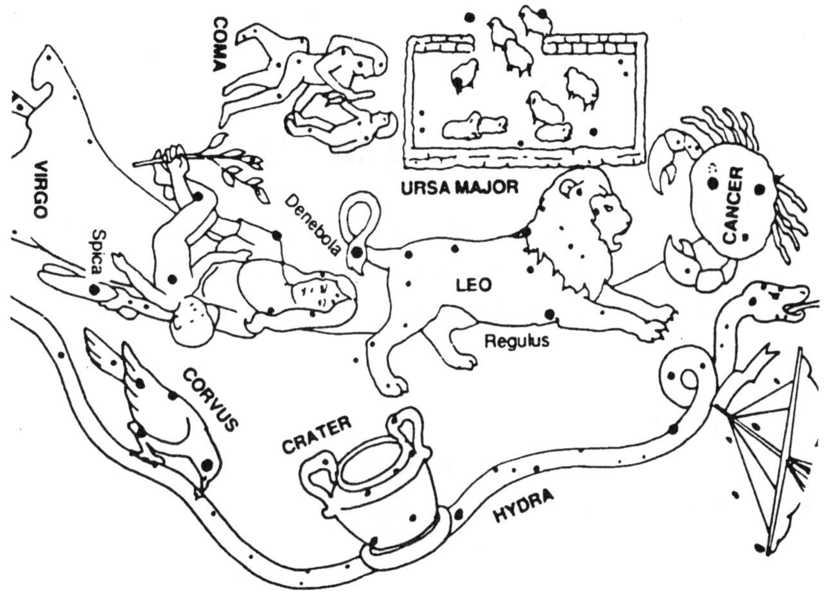

Chapter Fifteen

Leo (The Lion)

The twelfth and last sign is *Leo* and is shown as a full grown lion leaping up, about to jump on his enemy Hydra, the serpent. Jesus is called a lion in Revelation 5:5:

> *Then one of the elders said to me, "Do not weep! See, the Lion of the tribe of Judah, the Root of David, has triumphed. He is able to open the scroll and its seven seals."*

The Hebrews called this sign *Arieh*, "the lion tearing or rending." The Arabs called him *Al Asad*, "the lion who rends." This sign speaks of the wrath and judgment of God.

Leo ends the last act of the heavens, and you will notice that Leo and Taurus form what appears to be bookends in this last section of the sky. Both Taurus and Leo represent the wrath of God.

The Star Names of Leo

The brightest star in this sign is *Regulus* (Hebrew), meaning "the treading underfoot." Here we see the end of the prophecy of Genesis 3:15. Other stars are *Denebola*, "the judge or Lord who comes quickly"; *Al Giebha,* "the exaltation"; and *Al Dafera,* "the enemy put down." The names of this sign all reveal the message found in the book of Revelation, and the following decans tell the story with great accuracy.

Hydra (The Serpent)

The first decan of Leo is *Hydra* and means "the abhorred." It is shown as a long serpent who is being torn to pieces by Leo the Lion. A large cup is on his back and a bird is pecking and eating his flesh. This character has always represented evil, and the Persians called this "the serpent of Eve."

The Star Names of Hydra

The brightest star in Hydra is *Al Phard* (Arabic), "the excluded or put out of the way." Another star that is Arabic was called *Minchir Al Sugia,* "the tearing to shreds of the deceiver." Who is the deceiver?

> *And the great dragon was cast out, that old serpent, called the devil and Satan, which deceiveth the whole world: he was cast out into the earth, and his angels were cast out with him* (Revelation 12:9 KJV).

This sign clearly reveals the "putting out of the way" and the "tearing to pieces" of the "serpent of Eve."

Crater (The Cup)

The second decan of Leo is *Crater*, and is pictured as a cup. In some zodiacs, it is pictured pouring something out on the serpent. This cup represents the pouring out of the wrath of God. Let's look at what the Bible says about this:

> *A third angel followed them and said in a loud voice: "if any one worships the beast and his image and receives his mark on the forehead or on the hand, he, too, will drink of the wine of God's fury, which has been poured full strength into the cup of his wrath. He will be tormented with burning sulfur in the presence of the holy angels and of the Lamb"* (Revelation 14:9-10).

> *The seventh angel poured out his bowl into the air, and out of the temple came a loud voice from the throne, saying "It is done"* (Revelation 16:17).

> *The great city split into three parts, and the cities of the nations collapsed, God remembered Babylon the Great and gave her the cup filled with the wine of the fury of his wrath* (Revelation 16:19).

These are just a few of many examples found in the Bible. The Hebrews called this *Al Ches,* "the cup." There are no other names preserved for us in this sign.

Corvus (The Raven)

The last and final decan of Leo is *Corvus*, which is seen on the back of Hydra with its claws in the serpent, while at the same time he is pecking at the back of the serpent. Corvus is a raven, a scavenger and bird of prey. Ravens are very big and powerful, and have three inch beaks with which to tear at the flesh of dead animals. The final destruction of Satan and his forces are described in the following scripture:

> *And I saw an angel standing in the sun, who cried in a loud voice to all the birds flying in midair, "Come, gather together for the great supper of God, so that you may eat the flesh of kings, generals, and mighty men, of horses and their riders, and the flesh of all people, free and slave, small and great." Then I saw the beast and the kings of the earth and their armies gathered together to make war against the rider on the horse and his army. But the beast was captured, and with him the false prophet who had performed the miraculous signs on his behalf. With these signs he had deluded those who had received the mark of the beast and worshiped his image. The two of them were thrown alive into the fiery lake of burning sulphur. The rest of*

them were killed with the sword that came out of the mouth of the rider on the horse, and all the birds gorged themselves on their flesh (Revelation 19:17-21).

The next verses describe what happens to Satan:

And I saw an angel coming down out of heaven, having the key to the Abyss and holding in his hand a great chain. He seized the dragon, that ancient serpent, who is the devil, or Satan, and bound him for a thousand years. He threw him into the Abyss, and locked and sealed it over him, to keep him from deceiving the nations anymore until the thousand years were ended. After that, he must be set free for a short time (Revelation 20:1-3).

This story ends positively for the Christian in the next verse.

I saw thrones on which were seated those who had been given authority to judge. And I saw the souls of those who had been beheaded because of their testimony for Jesus and because of the Word of God. They had not worshipped the beast or his image and had not received his mark on their foreheads or their hands. They came to life and reigned with Christ a thousand years (Revelation 20:4).

The Star Names of Corvus

The brightest star in this sign is called in Hebrew *Al Chiba*, "the curse inflicted." The last star was named in Arabic *Minchir Al Gorab*, and means "the raven piercing," or "tearing to pieces." This raven harmonizes with Leo who is also seen as tearing and rending the serpent. Nothing more needs to be said. It is obvious that Leo and all his decans symbolize the wrath and judgement of God on the enemy and all who are his.

Conclusion

Now you have read the hidden message in the stars that God has declared to all the world. (Remember Psalm 19.) God hung these signs or banners in the heavens to tell the plan of redemption through Jesus Christ. The prophetic Word of God and the Zodiac tell the same story. Its most up-to-date message in the new star is that Jesus is coming soon. It is my prayer that you will be ready to meet the Lord in the air as page 112 describes. For more information on how to become a "born again" Christian, see page 122.

APPENDIX

How To Become a "Born Again" Christian

1) Realize you are a sinner and need the Savior Jesus. (We saw this in Libra.)
2) Realize you need to repent (change your mind).
3) Call upon the Lord to save you and forgive you.

For, everyone who calls on the name of the Lord will be saved (Romans 10:13).

Take time right now to pray to Him and ask Him to save you. Obey the following scripture:

That if you confess with your mouth "Jesus is Lord," and believe in your heart that God raised him from the dead, you will be saved. For it is with your heart that you believe and are just justified, and it is with your mouth that you confess and are saved (Romans 10:9-10).

Now read your Bible and attend a Bible believing church so you can become a disciple of Jesus. Lastly, share Jesus with other people so they can escape the wrath of God, too! You can show them this book about the stars and it will help you witness about Jesus.

The 12 Signs of the Zodiac & the 12 Tribes of Israel

1) Virgo is associated with the tribe of Zebulon.
2) Libra is associated with the tribe of Levi.

3) Scorpio is associated with the tribe of Dan.
4) Saggitarius is associated with the tribe of Asher.
5) Capricornus is associated with the tribe of Nephtali.
6) Aquarius is associated with the tribe of Reuben.
7) Pisces is associated with the tribe of Simeon.
8) Aries is associated with the tribe of Gad.
9) Taurus is associated with the tribe of Joseph.
10) Gemini is associated with the tribe of Benjamin
11) Cancer is associated with the tribe of Issachar.
12) Leo is associated with the tribe of Judah.

ABOUT THE AUTHOR

F. Chris Patrick has done evangelistic work in Haiti, Mexico, and Russia. He is the Director of both Wings of Life Ministries and Dove Ministries in Mobile, AL. Wings of Life ministers to those battling addictions.

The author is best known for writing books and tracts for the purpose of evangelism and training the Body of Christ in soulwinning.

For more information:
Dove Foundation
1567 Eslava St.
Mobile, AL 36604

CETUS
ERIDANUS
LEPUS
ORION
CANIS MAJOR
CANIS MINOR
DORADO
RETICULUM
SUPER NOVA 1987-A
ARGO
TAURUS
ARIES
GEMINI
PERSEUS
AURIGA
CANCER
PISCES
ANDROMEDA
CASSIOPEIA
CEPHEUS
URSA MINOR
URSA MAJOR
LEO
Regulus
HYDRA
CRATER
PISCES AUSTRALIS
PEGASUS
CYGNUS
DRACO
HERCULES
COMA
AQUARIUS
DELPHINUS
CAPRICORN
AQUILA
SAGITTA
LYRA
Vega
CORONA
CORVUS
Arcturus
Spica
BOOTES
VIRGO
SERPENS
SAGITTARIUS
LIBRA
CENTAURUS
OPHIUCHUS
Antares
SCORPIO
LUPUS
CRUX
ARA